ALSO BY NORMAN PODHORETZ

The
Present Danger

"DO WE HAVE THE WILL TO REVERSE
THE DECLINE OF AMERICAN POWER?"

Norman Podhoretz

A TOUCHSTONE BOOK
Published by Simon & Schuster, Inc.
NEW YORK

First Touchstone Edition, 1986

Published by Simon & Schuster, Inc.
Simon & Schuster Building
Rockefeller Center
1230 Avenue of the Americas
New York, New York 10020

TOUCHSTONE and colophon are registered trademarks
of Simon & Schuster, Inc.

Designed by Eve Metz

Manufactured in the United States of America

10 9 8 7 6 5 4 3 2 1 Pbk.

Library of Congress Cataloging in Publication Data

Podhoretz, Norman.
    The present danger.

    Includes bibliographical references.
    1. United States—Foreign Relations—Russia.
2. Russia—Foreign Relations—United States.
3. Russia—Foreign Relations—1975-
4. United States—Foreign Relations—1977-
I. Title.
E183.8.R9P6   327.73047   80-16435

ISBN 0-671-62866-6 Pbk.

Grateful acknowledgment is made for permission to reprint material from the
following articles:
"The Present Danger" by Norman Podhoretz, copyright © 1980 by
Commentary. Reprinted by permission.
"Making the World Safe for Communism" by Norman Podhoretz, copyright ©
1976 by Commentary. Reprinted by permission.
"The Culture of Appeasement" by Norman Podhoretz, copyright © 1977 by
Harper's Magazine. Reprinted by permission.
"The New Nationalism and the Election" by Norman Podhoretz, copyright ©
1980 by Public Opinion. Reprinted by permission.

To Neal Kozodoy

Contents

Preface to the New Edition

This book was written and originally published in what turned out to be the last year of the Carter administration and before it had become clear that Ronald Reagan would succeed Jimmy Carter as President of the United States. For a brief moment after the election of Reagan, it looked as though the struggle I describe in the pages that follow between "the culture of appeasement" and "the new nationalism" might finally be settled in favor of the new nationalism. But that was not to be, and by now, at the midpoint of Ronald Reagan's second term, these two great forces have fought their way to a stalemate. The battleground, of course, keeps shifting. In 1980 it was Iran and Afghanistan; in 1986, as this book is being reprinted, it is Central America and the Strategic Defense Initiative. Nevertheless, the underlying issues have remained unchanged, and the outcome also remains in doubt. Accordingly, "the present danger" of 1980 is still present today, and the question of whether "we have the will to reverse the decline of American power" still hangs as ominously as it did then in the troubled American air.

New York
Spring 1986

The Present Danger

On November 4, 1979, the day the American embassy in Teheran was seized and the hostages were taken, one period in American history ended; and less than two months later, on December 25, when Soviet troops invaded Afghanistan, another period began.

The past being easier to read than the present, we can describe the nature of the age now over with greater assurance than the one into which we are at this very moment just setting a hesitant and uncertain foot. Yet even to recognize whence we have come, let alone whither we are going, will require an effort to clear our minds of the cant that prevented an earlier understanding of the terrible troubles into which we were heading. I propose that we start, then, by renouncing the general idea that before Iran and Afghanistan we had moved from "cold war" to "détente" and that the old political struggle between "East" and "West" was yielding in importance to a new economic conflict between "North" and "South."

The assumptions behind this scheme have all been shattered by the events of the past few months, but they have served so well and for so long to disguise and deny the ominous consequences of a tilt in the balance of power from the United States to the Soviet Union that a fierce effort is being made to rescue them from discredit. If that effort should succeed, more would be lost than intellectual clarity. Indeed, I would go so far as to say that it would signify the final collapse of an American resolve to resist the forward surge of Soviet imperialism. In that case, we would know by what name to call the new era into which we have entered (though it would be an essential feature of that era that we would be forbidden to mention its name aloud): the Finlandization of America, the political and economic subordination of the United States to superior Soviet power.

1 · The Truman Doctrine and Containment

THE PERIOD usually called the cold war began in 1947 when the United States, after several years of acquiescence in the expansion of the Soviet empire, decided to resist any further advance, whether in the form of military invasion by Soviet troops or political subversion by local Communist parties. Up until this point the Russians had enjoyed a free hand. They had been permitted to occupy most of Eastern Europe and to begin installing puppet regimes in one after another of the countries of the region. Now, with Greece and Turkey threatened by the same fate, the United States finally began rousing itself from the semi-euphoric and semi-torpid state into which it had fallen at the end of World War II. In March 1947, announcing a special program of aid to Greece and Turkey, President Truman, in the doctrine soon to bear his name, declared that "it must be the policy of the United States to support free peoples who are resisting attempted subjugation by armed minorities or by outside pressure."

Within the next few months, the Marshall Plan was launched to aid in the reconstruction of the war-torn economies of Western Europe. Then came a Communist coup in Czechoslovakia, which destroyed the independence of another East European country and the only one with a democratic political system. Partly in response to a similar danger posed to Italy and France by huge local Communist parties subservient to Moscow, and partly to guard against an actual Soviet invasion of Western Europe, the North Atlantic Treaty Organization (NATO) was formed.

The name given to this two-sided politico-military strategy of American resistance to Soviet imperialism was containment, and it remained the guiding principle of American foreign policy until it was replaced two decades later, in 1969, by a new policy and a new presidential doctrine, bearing the name of Richard Nixon.

In one of the Orwellian inversions at which Soviet propaganda has always been so adept, this strategy of resistance, of holding a defensive line against their own imperialistic ambitions, the Russians described and stigmatized (in the words of *The Soviet Diplomatic Dictionary*) as a declaration of war by "the United States and . . . the imperialist military blocs" on "the Soviet Union and other Socialist States after the Second World War."

From that moment to this, any and every lowering of American resistance to Soviet imperialism has been praised by the Russians as a move away from the "cold war," and any sign of a reawakened concern, let alone of concrete action, has been denounced as a "return to the cold war."

Thanks to the process of what Fred Iklé has called "semantic infiltration," this Orwellian use of the term "cold war" has come into currency in the United States and in the West generally. Thus when the Soviet Union sent seventy-five thousand troops into Afghanistan and President Carter responded with expressions of alarm and a relatively mild series of countermeasures, most of them no more than symbolic, a whole rash of articles appeared in the American public prints denouncing the *United States* for this "capricious reversion to the cold war." [1]

"Here we go again," announced Richard J. Walton, a historian, on the op-ed page of *The New York Times*.[2] "The cold war, about to expire of old age, is rejuvenated"—not, in Mr. Walton's account, by the Soviet invasion of Afghanistan but by "American politicians" who even before the invasion "were beginning to run against the Russians." Mr. Walton assured us that he was "hardly suggesting that the Russians are beyond reproach," but it was the Americans who were "off to the cold war" once again.

In similar fashion, Alan Wolfe, writing in *The Nation*,[3] of whose editorial board he is a member, denounced Jimmy Carter for whipping up "cold-war hysteria" in order to win the election. According to Mr. Wolfe, "the invasion fits into an ongoing trend" not, evidently, within the Soviet Union but within the United States: "This is not the first time in the history of the cold war that the United States has begun to treat Russia as a hostile power, only to have the Russians act like one, thereby confirming American sentiment."

In *Newsweek*,[4] Robert Lasch, the former editor of

The St. Louis Post-Dispatch, added his voice to the chorus denouncing President Carter for "reviving the cold war," and doing so, like Truman before him, for no better reason than to "surmount a catastrophic decline in public esteem and win re-election by posing as a tough little rooster, ready to take on the Russians." As for the Soviet invasion of Afghanistan, "it is hardly surprising that the Soviet government, dreading an attack by the West, might decide to nail down the security of its frontiers by taking power in Afghanistan as it previously did in Eastern Europe." We might, Mr. Lasch acknowledged, have been "right to protest it in the United Nations." But there was certainly no need to overreact with hysterics.

Finally, the well-known economist and political commentator Robert Lekachman, while characterizing the Soviet invasion as "blundering," found stronger language with which to describe "the new cold-war fervor" in the United States: Congress, he said, was "enjoying a virulent case of raving patriotism." [5]

Obviously the term "cold war" is by now so charged with tendentious implications and so loaded with grotesquely unbalanced political judgments that it can no longer serve any serious intellectual purpose. The first thing to do, then, if we really wish to know where we have been, where we are, and where we are going, is to discard it in favor of "containment" when we talk about the role played by the United States in the first act of the great historical drama which opened in 1947.

2 · Mr. X

ALTHOUGH it was in the Truman Doctrine that the policy of containment was officially enunciated, it received its most authoritative expression in an article published in the July 1947 issue of *Foreign Affairs* under the title "The Sources of Soviet Conduct." [1] The author, identified at the time as "Mr. X," was George F. Kennan, the first director of the Policy Planning Staff of the State Department. About thirty years later, in what was perhaps the most dramatic single case of the loss of faith in containment caused by the experience of Vietnam, Kennan for all practical purposes repudiated the position he had taken in this article. Like many others of his generation, the great theorist of containment became what he himself called, with a candor few of the others had the courage or the audacity to match, a "semi-isolationist." But even to Kennan's admirable candor on these momentous issues there were limits. Thus he suggested that it was not so much that he had changed his mind about containment, as that his conception of it had been distorted in practice by an excessive emphasis on the military component of a strategy that he had envisaged as primarily political.

Yet anyone who reads "The Sources of Soviet Conduct" today is unlikely to come away with the impression that Kennan meant to stress the political over the military. His two main points, made not once but several times, are that the Soviet Union is embarked on a long-range strategy to overthrow the societies of the capitalist world and replace them with Communist regimes, and that this aim can only be frustrated by an equally determined strategy of resistance. Thus "the main element of any United States policy toward the Soviet Union must be that of a long-term, patient but firm and vigilant containment of Russian expansive tendencies." Or again: ". . . the Soviet pressure against the free institutions of the Western world is something that can be contained by the adroit and vigilant application of counter-force at a series of constantly shifting geographical and political points, corresponding to the shifts and maneuvers of Soviet policy, but which cannot be charmed or talked out of existence."

No doubt the "counter-force" Kennan had in mind was not exclusively military in nature. But there can be even less doubt that the American interventions into Korea and Vietnam were entirely consistent with his formulations. In fact, when we add to them the statement that the duty of "all good Communists" everywhere in the world "is the support and promotion of Soviet power, as defined in Moscow," we have to conclude that, in principle at least, Kennan's conception of containment imposed a prima facie requirement on the

United States to use military force in Korea and Vietnam. For in his view, in each of these cases an effort was being made to expand Soviet power through the expansion of Communist regimes serving Moscow's long-range purposes. That greater practical wisdom or tactical prudence would have counseled nonintervention into Vietnam—on the ground that the chances of success were so slight—says nothing about the principle, or about its applicability to situations where the local conditions might be more favorable to military action. Korea itself was the classic example of such a situation, and a test case of the seriousness of containment.

In the years between the enunciation of the policy and the outbreak of the Korean War, the United States had given containment concrete expression in the formation of NATO, and in a variety of actions designed to deter any advance of Soviet power beyond the lines established at the end of World War II and thus far crossed only by the coup in Czechoslovakia (for which, perhaps, the defection of Communist Yugoslavia was regarded as an even trade). At first there had been opposition to the new policy from the Left as well as the Right. On the Left, the argument was that the Soviet Union—in contrast to what the theory of containment supposed—was pursuing a defensive rather than an aggressive policy, and that Stalin wanted only security and peace. On the Right, the theory of Soviet intentions lying behind containment was accepted, but the prescription for American policy was attacked as overly defensive. Whereas the Left advocated disarmament and "understanding," the Right demanded "rollback" and liberation. It was not enough to hold out the hope, as

Kennan did, of promoting "tendencies which must eventually find their outlet in either the breakup or the gradual mellowing of Soviet power"; the East European satellites had to be helped to rise up and rebel against their Soviet masters.

Yet neither of these two opposing assaults on containment could make much headway in the early years. The left-wing attack organized itself in Henry Wallace's campaign for the presidency in 1948 and was so badly humiliated at the polls (Wallace receiving not the ten million votes he had expected but only about a million) that it sank into oblivion as a political force. In the world of ideas, too, the benign interpretation of Soviet intentions suffered a severe pounding at the hands of critics who could point both to Soviet doctrine and to Soviet action in refuting the view that Stalin was interested only in security and peace.

As for the attack from the Right, it turned out to be more rhetorical than real. Thus when—encouraged by a Republican administration in which John Foster Dulles and Richard Nixon, two of the leading critics of containment from the Right, served in high positions—the Hungarians rose up against their Soviet masters, the United States looked on sympathetically but took no action.

The Korean War had also broken out as a result of American encouragement. In that case, however, it was the Communists we encouraged, in the form of an announcement by Secretary of State Dean Acheson seeming to suggest that the defense of South Korea was not a vital American interest. Whether Acheson thus misled the Soviet Union and its North Korean clients by inadvertence, or whether the United States changed its mind at the sight of Communist troops actually invading a non-Communist nation, the American decision to hold the line against any further expansion of Soviet or Communist power was virtually unhesitant. We went to war; and in doing so we demonstrated in unmistakable terms that we were serious about the "application of counter-force at a series of constantly shifting geographical and political points, corresponding to the shifts and maneuvers of Soviet policy"—that is, about containment.

At the same time, the way we fought the war in Korea became a first clear indication that the critics of containment from the Right—for all that they seemed to have one of the two major parties behind them—were to be no more influential in the shaping of American policy than the critics on the Left. In refusing to do more in Korea than repel the North Korean invasion, or, as Truman put it, "to restore peace there and to restore the border," [2] a policy which his critics on the Right denounced as appeasement and timidity, the United States served notice on the world that it had no intention of going beyond containment to rollback or liberation.

Any lingering doubt as to whether this was the policy of the United States rather than the policy of the Democratic party was removed when the Republicans came into office in 1953 under Eisenhower. Far from adopting a bolder or more aggressive strategy, the new President ended the Korean War on the basis of the status quo ante—in other words, precisely on the terms of containment. And when, three years later, he refrained from going into Hungary, he made it correlatively clear that while the United States would resist the expansion of Soviet power by any and every means up to and including war, it would do nothing—not even provide aid to colonies of the Soviet empire seeking national independence and wishing to throw in their political lot with the democratic world—to shrink the territorial dimensions of Soviet control.

In reality, if not entirely in rhetoric, then, there was a bipartisan consensus behind the policy of containment as outlined by Kennan in "The Sources of Soviet Conduct." But even putting it that way understates the case. The fact is that there was a *national* consensus which went deeper than the realm of electoral politics. Nor did this consensus express itself only in the negative terms of a weakening of the critics of containment from the Left and the Right. There was a positive dimension, caught by Kennan in the peroration of his article with an eloquent flourish that fully matched the magisterial brilliance of the analysis on which it rested:

The thoughtful observer of Russian-American relations will find no cause for complaint in the Kremlin's challenge to American society. He will rather experience a certain gratitude for a Providence which, by providing the American people with this implacable challenge, has made their entire security as a nation dependent on their pulling themselves together and accepting the responsibilities of moral and political leadership that history plainly intended them to bear.

In "pulling themselves together" precisely for these reasons and in this way, the American people experienced a surge of self-confident energy. Instead of the depression which had been expected in the postwar years, there was unprecedented prosperity, and its fruits were being more widely shared than anyone had ever dreamed possible. Millions upon millions of people with low expectations of life found themselves being offered opportunities to improve their lot; in response they worked, they produced, they built, they bred. Even many intellectuals—so recently "alienated" and marginal—joined in what was petulantly derided by the few remaining socialists among them as the "celebration" of America. Yet instead of resulting in a diminution of creativity, this new ethos generated a more exciting literature than the thirties before it or the sixties which would follow. (I think of the emergence in the fifties of such writers who shared in the newly positive attitude toward American society as Saul Bellow, Ralph Ellison, William Styron, Robert Lowell, John Berryman, Lionel Trilling, Reinhold Niebuhr, Hannah Arendt, and George Kennan himself.)

In addition to "pulling themselves together" in this way, the American people also realized Kennan's hope that they would accept "the responsibilities of moral and political leadership that history plainly intended them to bear." They accepted these responsibilities by supporting the Marshall Plan, possibly the most generous program of economic aid the world had ever seen, and by their willingness to pay the price in blood and treasure of policies designed to hold the line against a totalitarian system which had already destroyed any possibility of freedom in large areas of the globe and aimed to extend its barbarous reign over as much of the rest as it could. For this, too, they were rewarded by an upsurge of pride and self-confidence. It was a nation that believed itself capable of assuming leadership in the cause of defending freedom against the threat of totalitarianism. By the end of the decade, when John F. Kennedy succeeded Eisenhower as President, only a small minority of people on the Left doubted that the cause was just or that the will and the means to fight for it were there.

3 · Enter Vietnam

So MANY Democrats, including the vast majority who served in the upper echelons of the Kennedy administration, have by now repudiated or quietly drifted away from their earlier views that it seems necessary to stress what would otherwise be self-evident about the Kennedy administration: that it was, if anything, more zealous in its commitment to containment than the Eisenhower administration had been. Kennedy ran against his Republican opponent, Nixon, who had of course served as Eisenhower's Vice-President, on a platform charging that the Republicans had neglected our defenses (allowing a "missile gap" to develop between the United States and the Soviet Union) and that they were, moreover, softer on Communism than he was. (Nixon later came to believe that a major factor in his narrow defeat was Kennedy's success in establishing this point—improbable though it may sound to the ears of a later generation which knew not John—during one of their television debates.) [1]

Once in office, Kennedy and his Secretary of Defense, Robert McNamara, took immediate steps to move away from the Republican strategic doctrine of "massive retaliation"—according to which the United States would respond to any act of Communist aggression with a nuclear strike against the Soviet Union—toward a more flexible posture. As early as 1950, a group of professors from Harvard and MIT (including future members of the Kennedy administration like McGeorge Bundy, Carl Kaysen, Jerome Wiesner, Arthur Schlesinger, Jr., and John Kenneth Galbraith) had warned that the emphasis on nuclear weapons "provided the United States with no effective answer to limited aggression except the wholly disproportionate answer of atomic war. As a result it invited Moscow to use the weapons of guerrilla warfare and internal revolt in marginal areas in the confidence that such local activity would incur only local risks." [2] Kennedy himself picked up this theme eight years later, and his call as a senator for a military posture that could respond to such threats as "limited brushfire wars, indirect non-overt aggression, intimidation and subversion, internal revolution," [3] he answered with his policies as President. Among those policies were the attempted invasion of Cuba in the Bay of Pigs and the decision to send American "advisers" and then actual troops into Vietnam.

Although a universally acknowledged disaster, the Bay of Pigs did little to discredit the strategy of containment in general. It was taken as a great tactical blunder and written off as an unfortunate but perhaps necessary stage in the education of a new and inexperienced President. The decision to go into Vietnam, however, was to have much more radical consequences. In principle, to repeat the point once again, this decision was unremarkable. It followed upon the precedent of Korea in the sense that Vietnam, too, was a country partitioned into Communist and non-Communist areas and where the Communists were trying to take over the non-Communists by force. The difference was that whereas in Korea the North had invaded the South with regular troops, in Vietnam the aggression was taking the form of an apparently internal rebellion by a Communist faction. Very few people in the United States believed that the war in Vietnam was a civil war, but even if they had, it would have made little difference. For whatever the legalistic definition of the case might be, there was no question that an effort was being mounted in Vietnam to extend Communist power beyond an already established line. As such, it represented no less clear a challenge to containment than Korea.

The question, then, was not whether the United States ought to respond; the only question was whether the United States had the means to do so effectively. But given the fact that the new strategic doctrine of the Kennedy administration had been conceived precisely for the purpose of meeting just such a challenge ("indirect non-overt aggression, intimidation and subversion, internal revolution"), it was all but inevitable that Kennedy's answer should be yes. The only dissent from this answer within his administration came from those who argued that military measures would fail unless we also forced the South Vietnamese government to undertake programs of liberal reform. But this argument implicitly called for a greater degree of American intervention than the dispatch of troops alone (and led eventually to the assassination of Diem and the assumption of complete American responsibility for the war).

A case might have been made—and indeed was made, by Hans J. Morgenthau, among others, outside the administration itself—against American intervention into Vietnam on the ground that the chances of success were too slight and the consequences of failure too great. As Morgenthau saw it, there was nothing wrong with trying to save South Vietnam from Communism, let alone with the strategy of containment in general; what was wrong was the tactical judgment, the attempt to apply a sound policy in an inappropriate and unfavorable situation. Morgenthau added that if we allowed ourselves to get dragged into an interminable war in South Vietnam —which we would be unable to win in any case—it would have the same kind of divisive effects on our society as the Algerian war had had on the French. The interests at stake in Southeast Asia were simply not vital enough to justify the risk.[4]

Sound, and even irrefutable, as this analysis seems in retrospect, it commanded very little assent in official Washington. There the prevailing conviction was that we now had the kinds of counterinsurgency forces required to save South Vietnam from Communism, and there was also what can only be called an itch to test out the new techniques.

But if the only question raised by Vietnam in the early days was the tactical one of whether it was possible for intervention to succeed, more fundamental questions began to be raised as the war dragged on. Whether or not the intervention could succeed, was it necessary or desirable? One of the main assumptions behind containment was that any advance of Communist power amounted to an expansion of Soviet power, but was that necessarily true? Might this not be a case of Chinese expansionism? If so, given the ever widening rift between the Russians and the Chinese, in what sense did American resistance fall under the imperative of containing Soviet expansionism? And if we were now faced with a separate problem of Chinese expansionism, was a mechanical application of the same strategy we had developed to counter the Soviet imperial thrust the best way to deal with it? Or again: might the war in Vietnam actually be an internal Vietnamese affair—a case of covert aggression from the North with local purposes of its own (the unification of the country, and perhaps domination of the whole region, by Hanoi) having little to do with either Soviet or Chinese power? Or finally, might it be an entirely internal *South* Vietnamese affair—a civil war of real significance to no one but the people of that country?

Obviously the rationale for American intervention into Vietnam depended on clear answers to such questions. Yet they were never forthcoming. Or rather, the ground of our policy kept shifting as the years wore on. First we were countering Soviet expansionism, then we were drawing a line in Asia against Chinese expansionism similar to the one we had drawn in Europe against the Russians, then we were fighting to preserve the independence of a friendly country which had been invaded by another, and finally we were preserving the credibility of our commitments to allies in other parts of the world.

In short, to the casualties in blood of the Vietnam War was added another casualty—the loss of clarity which had marked the policy of the United States for twenty years through Democratic and Republican administrations alike.

Nor was this the only wound suffered by containment in Vietnam. There was also a loss of confidence in the ability of the United States to discharge "the responsibilities of moral and political leadership." In saying that "history plainly intended" the United States to bear those responsibilities, Kennan (no American chauvinist, to put it mildly) surely had in mind not some inherent virtue in the American character but the predominance of sheer power with which history, working through two world wars that had finally exhausted the energies of Western Europe, had left the United States. Despite all the talk, friendly or hostile, about American "arrogance" or the "illusion of American omnipotence," this power was not exercised by Americans as though they thought it was absolute. If they really had entertained any such arrogant illusion of omnipotence, they would surely have refused to tolerate Soviet domination of Eastern Europe or the capture of mainland China by the Communists at a time when America enjoyed a nuclear monopoly. But it would on the other side be foolish to deny that before Vietnam, American confidence in American power was very great—not unlimited but great. Anything within reason we wanted to do we believed we had the power to do. This confidence in American power was the second major casualty of the defeat in Vietnam.

As with power, so with "moral and political leadership." If at the beginning domestic criticism of our military intervention into Vietnam was restricted to tactical issues, and if toward the middle the political wisdom of the intervention came into very serious question, by the end the moral character of the United States was being indicted and besmirched. Large numbers of Americans, including even many of the people who had led the intervention in the Kennedy years, were now joining the tiny minority on the Left who had at the time denounced them for stupidity and immorality, and were now saying that going into Vietnam had progressed from a folly to a crime. No greater distance could have been traveled from the original spirit of containment, reaffirmed in such ringing tones in John F. Kennedy's inaugural address ("Let every nation know, whether it wishes us well or ill, that we shall pay any price, bear any burden, meet any hardship, support any friend, oppose any foe, to assure the survival and the success of liberty"), than to this new national mood of self-doubt and self-disgust. The domestic base on which containment had rested was gone.

4 · The Nixon Doctrine

It was in response to this new political reality that a Republican administration, coming into office under Richard Nixon a little more than twenty years after containment was first enunciated, decided to begin moving away from it and toward a new international role for the United States. In a process not unfamiliar to other countries and other conservative leaders (France under de Gaulle, Israel under Begin), Nixon, who had once denounced containment as "cowardly" and would in the past have been expected to abandon it if at all in favor of a more aggressive stance, moved instead in the other direction—toward withdrawal, retrenchment, disengagement.

As getting into Vietnam had served under Kennedy and Johnson to discredit the old strategy of containment, getting out of Vietnam would now—so Nixon and his National Security Adviser, Henry Kissinger, thought—become the model or paradigm of a new strategy of retreat. American forces were to be withdrawn from Vietnam gradually enough to permit a build-up of South Vietnamese power to the point where the South Vietnamese could assume responsibility for the defense of their own country. The American role would then be limited to supplying the necessary military aid. The same policy, suitably modified according to local circumstances, would be applied to the rest of the world as well. In every major region, the United States would now depend on local surrogates (including Communist China—hence the opening to it—and of course Iran under the Shah) rather than on its own military power to deter or contain any Soviet-sponsored aggression. We would supply arms and other forms of assistance, but from henceforth the deterring and the fighting would be left to others. Thus did the Truman Doctrine give way to the Nixon Doctrine, and containment to strategic retreat.

To be sure, the new policy did not call itself by any such unattractive name as "strategic retreat." It was called "détente" and it was heralded as the beginning of a new era in the relations between the United States and the Soviet Union. In this new era, a "structure of peace" would be built, with cooperation between the two superpowers replacing "confrontation." Negotiations would proceed to limit the proliferation of strategic nuclear weapons; and the Americans and the Russians would also agree to exercise restraint in their dealings with third parties so as to lessen the danger that they might be drawn into direct conflict with each other.

To the critics of "détente" it was clear at the time, as it has become clear to almost everyone in retrospect, that the new strategy rested on the highly questionable

33

assumption that the Soviet Union could be contained by any force other than American power. Nixon and Kissinger believed—or perhaps only hoped against hope —that a combination or "linkage" of surrogate force and positive economic and political incentives would be enough to restrain Soviet adventurism; and where this combination proved insufficient, a serious show of American determination (such as the calling of a nuclear alert during the Yom Kippur War of 1973 in response to a threat of Soviet intervention on the side of Egypt) would make up the lack.

In other words, in their conception of it, "détente" was the highest degree of containment compatible with the post-Vietnam political climate in the United States —a climate in which Congress, supported by the leading centers of opinion within the foreign-policy establishment and the major news media, wanted only to cut back drastically on defense spending and to curtail American commitments abroad to a sparse minimum.

That this was indeed the climate in the Nixon years cannot be seriously questioned. In 1972, for example, the Brookings Institution suggested a $12.5 billion cutback in defense programs (out of a budget of $76.5 billion). Senator Hubert Humphrey endorsed the proposal, while Senator George McGovern declared it inadequate and called for a $30 billion reduction instead. (Later, under the exigencies of his campaign for the presidency, McGovern agreed to settle for a $10 billion reduction.) *The New York Times* also thought that the $12.5 billion cut might be too modest, and devoted a sympathetic editorial [1] to a more radical Brookings plan amounting to what the *Times* characterized as "major surgery." (Brookings considered it more politic to describe its plan as the "elimination of less effective forces and a selective slowdown in modernization.")

The Brookings plan, said the *Times* approvingly,

> would eliminate half the strategic bomber and land-based ICBM forces and most air defense. The Navy would lose four of its sixteen carrier task forces and most of its ship-building program, the Air Force its chief new tactical air development, the F-15 fighter, and the Army, six active brigades plus some of its swollen support forces.

Nor was this enough:

> Bigger savings may be possible in strategic forces by halting deployment of the MIRV multiple warhead missiles, Minuteman III and Poseidon, slowing down development of the ULMS-Trident long-range missile submarine and shifting to a cheaper strategic bomber to replace the projected B-1.

Nor was this enough:

> But deep cutbacks in military spending must address themselves to conventional forces, which absorb more than three-fourths of the defense budget.

Nor was even all this enough:

> What can be given a close, hard look now . . . is the Pentagon's continuing acquisition of weapons systems, many of them over-sophisticated. . . . The Army's 10,000 helicopters, the Navy's unnecessary amphibious forces and the Air Force's deep-penetration tactical fighters are prime candidates, along with vulnerable $1-billion nuclear carriers, bomber defenses and support units.

35

A few weeks later,[2] the *Times* made the philosophy behind these recommendations altogether explicit:

We believe that the Nixon Administration, in its preoccupation with military might, has grievously misjudged America's national security needs in the 1970's. Not only that: the weapons build-up envisaged by this Administration would be wasteful of resources and inherently self-defeating. It would actually detract from American security by heightening suspicions and triggering countermeasures by the Soviet Union.

At a moment when the American defense budget was already beginning to decline in both relative and real terms, while the Soviet Union was forging grimly ahead (this, and not a reciprocal policy of restraint, was the only Soviet countermeasure triggered by our actions), the *Times* concluded:

America's defense budget is exploding, becoming in itself a threat to the security and well-being of the nation.

It was because of this kind of thing that Kissinger evidently came to believe that the United States had suffered a failure of nerve and no longer had the will or the stomach to pursue a serious strategy of containment. He also seems to have believed that the Soviet Union had entered a period of imperial dynamism. His role, like that of Metternich when confronted with the impending collapse of the monarchical system in the face of a rising democratic challenge, was to delay the inevitable for as long as possible. To win time was desirable in itself, and there was in any case a chance that unexpected developments might occur to change the entire picture.

Unfortunately for this conception, the only unexpected developments that actually did occur tended to undermine its viability as a modified strategy of containment. One such development was the failure of what had been the paradigmatic testing ground of the new strategy in Vietnam, where the new idea of containment through surrogate power followed the old idea of containment through American power into an early grave (though the obsequies were not read until four years later, after the fall of the Shah). In the case of Vietnam, not only was the surrogate power unable to hold the line on its own, but in the event, the United States refused even to provide it with the promised aid to defend itself against a military invasion encouraged and supplied with massive quantities of Soviet arms. To make yet another of the many historical ironies generated by this story still more mordant, the "discredited" theory on which we originally went into Vietnam —that the victory of Communism there would be tantamount to an expansion of Soviet power—was vindicated after many detours in the end, as Communist Vietnam allied itself with the Soviet Union against China and then drove on to extend its rule over the whole of Indochina.

The even more "discredited" domino theory was thereby vindicated too—and not merely in Indochina. No sooner had Vietnam fallen than Soviet proxies in the form of Cuban troops appeared in Angola, and again the United States refused to respond. Kissinger and the new President, Gerald Ford, appealed to Congress for aid to the pro-Western faction in Angola, which was being overwhelmed by its Communist rivals with the help of the Cuban troops. But Congress (again supported by the most influential sectors of opinion) said no, and for good measure cut down an effort by the CIA to provide covert assistance to the anti-Communist forces as well. Within the next few years—extending into the new Democratic administration under Jimmy Carter—five more countries (Laos, Ethiopia, Mozambique, Afghanistan, and Cambodia) were taken over by factions supported by and loyal to the Soviet Union, while the United States looked complacently on.

5 · The Arms "Race"

Nor was this developing pattern of Soviet advance and American retreat confined to conflicts involving clients or allies. More ominously, it showed itself in the changing balance between the two superpowers themselves. On the tenth anniversary of the Cuban missile crisis of 1962, *The New York Times* said that "for all the terrible danger it posed, [the crisis] must, on balance, be judged a positive event"—having taught "all rational men" the lesson that "All nations will be safer when dependable steps have been taken to dismantle atomic arsenals and end this reliance on fear of annihilation as the great deterrent." [1] This was not, however, the lesson the Soviet leaders derived from the Cuban missile crisis. After being forced by American superiority in both strategic nuclear forces and naval forces in place to back down, the Soviet Union had decided that it would never again be placed in such a situation. In line with that decision, the Soviets had embarked not on a program to dismantle their atomic arsenals, but rather on a build-up in every category of military force—nuclear as well as conventional, on land, on sea, and in the air— that would turn out to be the greatest military build-up in the peacetime history of the world.

Yet despite all the easy talk, then and now, about an arms race, the United States responded to this relentless marathon not by running but by standing still and even slipping back. In 1979 alone, even after a minor reversal of the steadily downward trend of American military spending from 1970–76, the Soviets still outstripped the United States by about 50 percent; and through the entire decade of the seventies, in the critical area of strategic forces, the Soviets spent nearly three times as much as the United States.* In most categories of conventional military force, the Soviet Union had long enjoyed an advantage over the United States, but the balance was maintained by American superiority in the quality of our arsenal and the quantity of our strategic nuclear weapons. Yet Soviet advances in both quality and quantity were combining with American "restraint" (a word which more and more took on the character of a euphemism for unilateral disarmament) to wipe out that advantage.

As the critics of détente began pointing out with mounting alarm, if these tendencies were to continue, the overall balance of power between the Soviet Union and the United States would shift in favor of the Soviets. And as the Soviets themselves began pointing out with scarcely concealed glee, such a shift would be

---

* These figures are based on a CIA report.[2] It is worth noting that CIA estimates of Soviet military spending have usually been found to be too low, not too high.

translated into a greater measure of Soviet "influence" everywhere in the world. Influence could mean throwing their weight around politically in negotiations with the West; it could mean intimidating other countries by menacing shows of force; it could mean dispatching Cuban and East German proxies to intervene in Third World countries without fear of opposition or reprisal; it could—though this would come as a surprise even to those who expected the worst of the Soviet Union but who were aware of its almost legendary caution in send-ing its own troops outside the boundaries of its own em-pire—mean outright Soviet military invasion and occu-pation; and in the worst case, it could mean the kind of political control over Western Europe, Japan, and ulti-mately even the United States that had come to be known as Finlandization.

Far from expressing concern over the changing bal-ance of power between the United States and the Soviet Union, or worrying about the consequences it could and was indeed already beginning to have, the Carter ad-ministration seemed sanguine about it. In an obverse re-play of what happened with containment when Eisen-hower replaced Truman in 1953, the new Democratic administration which came into office behind Carter in 1977 continued and even accelerated the strategic re-treat begun under the Republicans. Carter, who had campaigned against a putatively bloated defense budget and promised to cut defense spending by $5 billion to $7 billion, found it impossible to keep that promise as President. He did, however, cancel or delay produc-tion of one new weapons system after another—the B-1 bomber, the neutron bomb, the MX, the Trident—while the Soviet Union went on increasing and refining its entire arsenal.

Nor was any great alarm sounded by the Carter administration over the escalation of activity by Soviet proxies in the Middle East and Africa. To many observers all this activity seemed part of a developing strategy to put the Soviets into a position of control over the oil of the Middle East or at least over the routes through which it was transported to Europe, Japan, and the United States. But to Andrew Young, Carter's ambassador to the UN—perhaps reasoning by analogy with the notion that Soviet achievement of nuclear parity was a necessary precondition for stabilizing the "arms race"—Cuban troops in Africa were a force for stability. As for the fear of Soviet encirclement of the Middle East, it was dismissed as paranoia by spokesmen both in the government and in the press.

6 · "Mature Restraint"

B UT IF in general terms the pre-Afghanistan policies of
the Carter administration were continuous with the
strategy of retreat inaugurated by the two Republican
administrations preceding it, there was also a major difference in conception and attitude. Whereas Nixon,
Ford, and Kissinger saw détente as an adaptation of
containment to a set of changing circumstances—the
best, in effect, one could now hope to do—the Carter
administration seemed to see no need for containment
at all.

Although Kissinger had on occasion flirted with the
notion that the Soviet Union was becoming a "status-
quo power," his net assessment was that it had entered
a period of imperial expansionism. With the Carter administration, it was just the opposite. The President or
his National Security Adviser, Zbigniew Brzezinski,
might point in an extremity to Soviet misbehavior. But
in statement after statement by the President himself,
his Secretary of State, his ambassador to the UN, his

leading expert on Soviet affairs, and his apologists in the universities and the press, the American people were told that the Soviet Union and the United States had, in Secretary Vance's phrase, "similar dreams and aspirations," and that the Soviets were pursuing the same objectives as we were—stability and peace.

To be sure—so this reading of the Soviets went—they were still primitive enough to think that military power was as important as it had been in the past. But with patient instruction from us—reinforced by lessons like their expulsion from Egypt—they would soon learn that the world had entered a new era, in which military power was becoming less and less useful as an instrument of policy. In the nuclear field, strategic superiority (as Henry Kissinger himself had said—though he would later change his mind) was meaningless, and if the Soviets should remain so immature as to try to achieve it, they would gain nothing for their pains but economic hardship. As for sending their proxies into other countries, they would soon find that this, too, was a species of anachronistic activity. For not all the Cuban troops or Soviet weapons in the world could prevail against the force of nationalism, which would bog them down in quagmires and then extrude them altogether, as had happened to us in our own foolish turn in Vietnam.

Underlying all these considerations was the idea that the East-West conflict—the struggle between the United States and the Soviet Union—was becoming obsolescent and that a new axis of conflict was being drawn between the North and the South. The issues in this new conflict were not political—that is, they did not involve a struggle between Communism and democracy; they were, rather, economic, pitting the poor nations of the South against the developed countries of the North. Just as dozens of formerly subjugated peoples had demanded their political place in the sun and achieved it by becoming sovereign nations, so these same peoples and others, too, were now demanding their rightful share of the goods of the earth through the creation of a new international economic order. Such demands could not be resisted by force—which was another proof of the growing obsolescence of military might—and the problem was still further complicated by the fact that not all the economic power was in the hands of the North.

These propositions had been given a tremendous boost toward the status of axiomatic truth by the success of OPEC in imposing an embargo on sales to the West during the Yom Kippur War of 1973 and then in quadrupling the price of oil overnight. It was not, however, until the Carter administration took office three years later that they achieved the status of official American policy. In his now notorious speech at Notre Dame in May 1977, the President said that the "threat of conflict with the Soviet Union has become less intensive" and that the greater threat to peace came from a world "one-third rich and two-thirds hungry."

The upshot was that there was no longer any need for containment—whether in the Trumanesque form of American military power or in the Nixonian modification of local surrogates supported by American arms. As Carter himself put it, "Historical trends have weakened the foundation" of the two principles which guided our foreign policy in the past: "a belief that Soviet expan-

45

sion was almost inevitable and that it must be contained."

Given this way of looking at the world, it was only to be expected that the Carter administration would react with "mature restraint" to the overthrow of the Shah of Iran. In the Notre Dame speech the President had said: "Being confident of our own future, we are now free of that inordinate fear of Communism which once led us to embrace any dictator who joined us in that fear. I'm glad that's being changed."

The Shah being a prime example of just such a dictator, he might well have seen the writing on the wall in these words, especially when to their moral disapproval was added the idea of the obsolescence of containment even in the milder form of the Nixon Doctrine—which had made of the Shah a "pillar" of American security in the Persian Gulf. If the Nixon Doctrine had remained in force, it would have called upon us to support the Shah in doing whatever was necessary to stave off a revolution which might or might not have been pro-Soviet but was certainly anti-American. Whether Richard Nixon himself would have had the stomach and the political base for such a policy—involving, as it would have done, American acquiescence in the massacre by Iranian troops of many thousands of demonstrators—is open to serious doubt. In any case, Richard Nixon was gone, and the doctrine bearing his name was not about to be rescued by a President who saw no need for it and even seems to have thought that the United States would be better off without allies like the Shah.

In this, however, the President was lagging behind a new stirring in the public mind. Even some of his academic sympathizers were disturbed by the fall of the Shah and the rise of the Ayatollah. This strange new force was not the kind of thing the opponents of the Shah in the United States had counted on. Andrew Young and Ramsey Clark might praise the Ayatollah as a saint and a great believer in human rights, but most people were unsettled by his violent outbursts against the United States and his evident determination to take Iran not forward into the future but backward into a past darker from their point of view than the regime of the Shah. And there were those who, while priding themselves on being as free of the inordinate fear of Communism as anyone in the Carter White House, nevertheless began wondering if the Islamic revolution in Iran might turn out to be the prelude to a Soviet takeover of some kind. In any event, it was now acknowledged by sympathetic critics of the Carter administration, like Stanley Hoffmann [1] of Harvard and James Chace [2] of *Foreign Affairs*, that there could be no substitute for American power in the Persian Gulf or perhaps anywhere else. Either we would have to depend on our own power to hold the Soviets back, or we would have to rely on the hope that they would be contained by their own prudence and by their fear of local resistance.

7 · The Collapse of Carter's Policy

BUT IF the Nixon Doctrine collapsed along with its pillar, the Shah, the twin pillars of Carter's foreign policy were soon to collapse as well, one of them onto the same rubble heap in the streets of Teheran, and the other smashed by Soviet tanks in the streets of Kabul.

The first of these pillars was the idea that no great risk was entailed by the retrenchment of American power. In the new order of things, according to this idea, we could afford to divest ourselves of instrumentalities like a covert capability for intervention by the CIA and a rapid deployment force. Within days after the hostages had been seized in Teheran, the humiliating helplessness of the United States had led even some public figures who formerly favored a radical retrenchment to demand a restoration of these capabilities.

But there was another, subtler aspect to this issue, which had to do not with the availability of particular instruments of force but with the post-Vietnam American reluctance to use force at all. Here, too, an element of continuity between the Carter administration and the Nixon-Ford-Kissinger years was concealed amid all the differences, both rhetorical and real. Thus the failure of the United States to take military action against OPEC in 1973–74 marked the beginning of a period in which militarily powerless parties were able without fear of retaliation to commit what would certainly in the past— even in the very recent past—have been regarded as acts of aggression and even war against the United States. It would be hard to prove that the Iranians who jeered at the impotence of the United States in 1979 had been emboldened by the message of American behavior in 1973. But it is harder still to believe that American passivity in the face of a threat to the very lifeblood of its civilization did not lead to the obvious conclusion that the United States had lost its nerve and could now be taken on with impunity. For if the United States was not prepared to use force to ensure its access to oil, for the sake of what could it be expected to do so?

The form in which this point came home to American public opinion was the contrast between the attack on our embassy in Teheran and the protection afforded the Soviet embassy there when a group of protesters tried to storm it after the invasion of Afghanistan. How was it, many people began to ask, that our embassies were sacked, and not only in Teheran, whereas Soviet embassies remained inviolate? Might it have something to do with a fear of Soviet retaliation as against the expectation that the United States would go to any lengths to avoid the use of force? Once the hostages were taken, there might be no way of getting them out safely by military action. But a vast number of Americans were now confirmed in or converted to the view that only the certain knowledge of retaliation could deter others from attempting the same thing again, and that only military power and the willingness to use it could prevent still others from aggressing in still other ways against the United States.

No sooner did its assumption concerning the utility of American military power collapse than the Carter administration found its ideas about the efficacy of Soviet military power disintegrating too. The President himself had only recently said that the negative effects of Soviet racism and atheism would lead of their own unaided weight to the defeat of Soviet aims in Africa, but the Russians evidently disagreed. They seemed to believe —on the basis of their experience in Hungary and Czechoslovakia—that such effects could be countered well enough by troops and tanks and planes both in Africa and in the Middle East.

Nor could the Carter administration take much comfort from the expectation of some of its supporters and apologists that Afghanistan would become a "quagmire" and soon administer the same lesson to the obdurate Soviets about the uselessness of military power that we had learned in Vietnam. There was no free public opinion in the Soviet Union to interfere with any military operation; there was no outside force supplying the kind and quantity of arms to the Afghan rebels that the Soviets themselves had given to the North Vietnamese and without which the "lesson" could never have been taught to the United States.

But the invasion of Afghanistan did more than destroy the administration's old ideas about the utility of force in Soviet dealings with the Third World. It shook the very foundation of the administration's conception of the Soviet Union in general. No matter how this extraordinary move was interpreted, it was not easily compatible with the notion that the Soviet Union had become a status-quo power. Even if, as some desperately reassuring voices maintained, the Russians were acting defensively—fearful of what would happen if a Muslim insurgency should overthrow a client state on their own border—there was no denying that the sending of Soviet —not Cuban or East German, but Soviet—troops to a country outside the Warsaw Pact represented a new stage of Soviet expansionism.

Nor could it be denied that the decision to risk political and possibly other forms of retaliation bespoke a new level of Soviet boldness. For again, even if it was true, as the reassuring voices maintained, that the Soviets had underestimated the degree of outrage the invasion would provoke both in the United States and in the Third World, they certainly must have known that there would be *some* degree of outrage.

In either case, the invasion could not be reconciled with the idea of the Soviet Union as highly prudent in its international conduct. Or rather, it could best be reconciled with this idea in the opposite sense from what the reassuring voices intended. That is, given the normal reluctance of the Soviets to take undue risks, and given also their belief—often reiterated by Brezhnev— that as the "relationship of forces" tipped in their favor, they would be entitled to a proportionate extension of their power and influence, the invasion of Afghanistan could only be seen as a vindication of those critics of détente who had been warning since the early seventies that the retreat of American power would open the way to Soviet adventurism and expansionism.

Finally, the invasion of Afghanistan persuaded the Carter administration that "North-South" had not yet quite replaced "East-West" as the central axis of conflict in our time. This idea had in any case always been dubious, smacking of a great desire to escape from the responsibilities of containment by proclaiming that there was no longer any need to exercise them. Moreover, even the distinction between East-West and North-South had always been problematic.

First of all, in its conflicts with the "South," the United States always had to worry about the possibility of a confrontation with the military might of the "East." This was true in 1973, when the last polemical resort against a forcible American takeover of the oil fields was the argument that the Russians might move in to prevent it; and it was true later in Africa, where, for example, the case against American backing of Bishop Abel Muzorewa in Zimbabwe Rhodesia was that such a policy might drag us into a war with the Cubans.

Secondly, despite protestations of neutrality, much of the "South" was for all practical purposes on the side of the "East" against the West. In their meeting in Havana in 1979, for example, the "nonaligned" nations passed a series of viciously anti-American resolutions and came close to following Cuba's lead into an alliance with the Soviet bloc—this after three years of punctilious nonintervention and positive wooing by the "imperialistic" United States while Cuban and East German troops and Soviet military advisers were busily absorbing countries throughout the "South" into the "East" by force.

That the ultimate objective of all this Soviet-inspired and -sponsored activity was extension of control by the "East" over that part of the "South" located in the Persian Gulf in order to gain political domination over the "West" (known for purposes of economics as the "North"), and also to ensure a source of oil for themselves as their own supplies began to dwindle, seemed clear to many observers long before the invasion of Afghanistan. But it became clear to the President of the United States only after the invasion of Afghanistan. It was then that Carter declared that "An attempt by any outside force to gain control of the Persian Gulf region will be regarded as an assault on the vital interests of the U.S." and that "It will be repelled by use of any means necessary, including military force."

Ten years after it was first proclaimed, then, the Nixon Doctrine gave way to the Carter Doctrine—a new version, or so it seemed, of the Truman Doctrine of old. If the President could be believed, the period of strategic retreat was over and a new period of containment had begun.

8 · The Carter Doctrine

AND so we come to the present moment and to the question of whether the President can be believed. The reasons for being skeptical are clear. The President himself is so recent a convert to these new ideas that doubts inevitably arise as to the seriousness of his commitment and his steadiness of purpose. Some ungenerous critics have wondered at whom the Carter Doctrine is really aimed: at the Soviet Union or at the American voters in an election year? Others have asked how the new policy can be effectively implemented by an administration still made up of the same people who until yesterday were pressing in a very different direction.

Yet even if such unkind speculations are dismissed and even if the President is given the benefit of every doubt, a far more ominous question arises. *Is it too late?*

For a long time now, groups like the Coalition for a Democratic Majority and the Committee on the Present Danger have been sounding the alarm over the deterioration of our defenses and the build-up of Soviet military capability. They have warned that these trends, if not reversed, would lead to the opening of a "window of opportunity" for the Soviet Union—a period in which military superiority would embolden the Soviets to move forward quickly, before the United States could correct the imbalance and slam the window shut. The date at which this window would open was generally estimated—with Orwell as an unconscious guide?—to be 1984. But the invasion of Afghanistan may mean that the Soviets think the window is open *now*.

If they do, they have every incentive to keep going— with their own troops, or by encouraging internal insurrections and coups, or by some combination of both— until they have the oil. Even the steps toward mobilization now announced by President Carter—increases in military spending, registration for the draft, and the like—might paradoxically strengthen their incentive to press on now, before we can pull ourselves together and shut the window again. This is the point to which ten years of retreat may have brought us: damned if we do, and damned if we don't.

In short, the arms "race" we have allegedly been running has now left the United States with virtually no means other than a threat of nuclear war to protect the lifeline and the lifeblood of our civilization. From everything we know about the Soviets, they will be deterred by that threat so long as the nuclear balance is even or in our favor. This is why the contention, advanced by Senator Edward M. Kennedy [1] among others, that "nuclear weapons like the MX" have no "relevance" to a "regional crisis" (!) like Afghanistan is dangerously wrong. If it is not already too late, and if we do get safely through the present crisis, we will only be delaying the inevitable unless we resolve now to use the additional time not only to restore our conventional capability but precisely to spend "the many billions more in defense systems" opposed by Kennedy but which alone can prevent the Soviets from achieving nuclear superiority and thus an unobstructed road to domination. The MX may or may not be the best such system we can buy, but there can be no question that at the very least we will need some new system—possibly the ABM—to make our Minuteman force invulnerable to a Soviet first strike.[2]

It may, as I say, already be too late. The Soviets may think that the nuclear balance has now tipped in their favor. Or they may think that the parity which we have deliberately permitted them to achieve over the past fifteen years (on the theory that it would satisfy them and lessen the danger of war) has deprived the American nuclear threat of credibility. If so, the superiority of their conventional forces to ours means that there is nothing to stop them now from advancing but the "Arab nationalism and the Muslim religious feeling" on which Senator Kennedy [3]—like President Carter in his pre-Afghanistan political incarnation—places his hopes. Yet the example of Afghanistan itself, where fierce nationalism and Muslim religious feeling have not exactly proved effective as "a powerful force against Soviet ambition," suggests that this is a frail reed indeed for us to lean upon.

Even if the Soviets should decide for one reason or another to pause, there is a danger that the finally aroused American giant will once again be lulled back to sleep. In that case, the Carter Doctrine could turn out to be nothing more than an insubstantial election-year slogan, and the nascent new effort of resistance to Soviet imperialism might be cut off in its infancy: the extra billions for defense would be canceled, and neither the MX nor any other such "irrelevant" system would be built. Meanwhile the Soviets would consolidate their gains, go on increasing and refining their arsenal, and wait for the window of opportunity to open even wider and lock itself permanently into position. Soon enough, perhaps by the date chosen by Orwell's prophetic soul—when to their political ambition to dominate the West would have been added the Soviets' own economic need for Middle Eastern oil—the President of the United States, whoever he might be, would have to choose between nuclear war or Soviet control over the oil supply of the West. By then the vulnerability of our missiles to a Soviet first strike would automatically dictate surrender—checkmate by telephone, as someone has called it.

9 · Finlandization

But whether now or then, what would surrender mean? What would the Finlandization of America look like?

In contrast to the traditional kind, this new species of surrender would not be accompanied by the arrival of Soviet troops or formalized in an unambiguous declaration. There would be no military occupation, and the closest thing to an announcement of surrender might be a speech by the President abrogating the Carter Doctrine in words similar to those already used in a letter published shortly after the invasion of Afghanistan in *The New York Times:* "Why . . . should we, at the risk of starting World War III, keep the Russians from displacing the present owners? They might be more efficient producers, and they might save us money by eliminating the corruption that is an element of the present price." [1] Such words would be applauded by "responsible" people, and they would represent the beginning of a gradual but steady process of accommodation to Soviet wishes and demands.

For example, to forestall a cutoff of oil, we would immediately shelve any plans for deploying the new theater nuclear weapons in Western Europe. Then various SALT agreements, entirely skewed in the Soviet favor but universally described as "mutual" and "balanced," would be negotiated. Trade agreements involving the transfer of technology, grain, and anything else the Soviets might want or need would also be negotiated on terms amounting to the payment of tribute, and with an inexorably commensurate decline in the American standard of living.

In countries like France and Italy, where huge Communist parties already exist, they would undoubtedly come to power, in all probability by democratic means. Indeed, many non-Communists would vote for them as the party most likely to represent the lightest form of Soviet domination—Red Vichy regimes whose loyalty to the foreign masters would make military occupation unnecessary and would preserve a minimal degree of national independence.

In the United States, where there is no Communist party to speak of, Finlandization would take a subtler political shape. Politicians and pundits would appear to celebrate the happy arrival of a new era of "peace" and "friendship" and "cooperation" between the Soviet Union and the United States. Dissenters from this cheerful view would be castigated as warmongers and ways would be found to silence questions and criticisms, which could, after all, only result in making things worse for everyone. Only those politicians would run who could be depended upon to support the terms on which the threat of nuclear war had finally been banished from the earth. Of course, such politicians would work toward a sociopolitical system more in harmony with the Soviet model than the "unjust" and "reactionary" system we have today.

There is no need to go on filling in the details. A world in which the Soviet Union had the military power to seize control of the oil fields would be a world shaped by the will and tailored to the convenience of the Soviet Union.

10 · Pacifism After Vietnam

Let us, however, suppose—let us pray—that it is not already too late. Will the American giant, so recently roused, be lulled back to sleep? No confident answer can be given to that question. Despite the Carter Doctrine and the energizing fears and passions that gave rise to it, the soporific forces among us remain powerful. There is, first and foremost, the American attitude toward war. The idea of war has never been as natural or as glamorous to Americans as it used to be to the English or the Germans or the French. We have always tended in this country to think of war as at best a hideous necessity, not as a "continuation of politics by other means" or, alternatively, as an opportunity for heroism, glory, and honor. War to Americans is a calamity when it happens, it is a dirty business while it lasts, and the sooner it can be gotten over with the better. But negative as this attitude may be, it is still a far cry from the undifferentiated fear, loathing, and revulsion that the prospect of war now seems to inspire in the American mind.

No doubt a rise in pacifist sentiment is inevitable in the wake of any war, especially a war that ends, as Vietnam did, in humiliation and defeat. No doubt, also, the way the war in Vietnam was reported as well as the way it was opposed (a distinction more easily made in theory than it was ever observed in practice) helped to stimulate a vaguely pacifist response. All one heard about and saw was the horrors of war—unredeemed, as it appeared, by any noble purpose. No heroes emerged, only villains and victims, and nothing good was accomplished by American troops and American arms; only evil: only destruction, misery, murder, and guilt.

This is how pacifist ideologues look upon war in general, and the prominent position of pacifist organizations in the protest movement against American military involvement in Vietnam probably influenced the way the war came to be conceived and described. (It is worth noting, however, that the pacifist world was split between those who, in the traditional pacifist spirit, regarded all wars as equally evil and those who, in a newer spirit, were willing to justify and even celebrate "wars of national liberation" and to condemn only "wars of imperialist aggression," such as they imagined the United States was waging in Vietnam.)

But be all that as it may, so powerful did the pacifist tide become that it even reached backward to engulf World War II, probably the most popular war in which the United States had ever participated. To this "Vietnamization" of World War II, as we may call it, two immensely successful novels of the sixties, Joseph

Heller's *Catch-22* and Kurt Vonnegut's *Slaughterhouse-Five*, made perhaps the largest contribution. Although written without reference to Vietnam and published in 1961, just before American troops began to be sent there, *Catch-22* achieved full cultic status only later in the decade, when it could be seized upon to discredit the one war from which something good had almost universally been thought to have come. Not even World War II, the war against Hitler, was worth fighting, said *Catch-22*, to the acclaim of millions; nor, added Vonnegut in his story of the bombing of Dresden, had we acted any less criminally in that war than we were acting in Vietnam.

As the past was thus Vietnamized, so are the present and the future now being subjected to the same treatment. Shortly after President Carter called for a resumption of draft registration, Senator Kennedy brought cheers from an audience of Harvard students when, in a blatant evocation of the imagery of Vietnam, he warned that war in the Persian Gulf would mean "a nightly television body count of America's children." [1] A day or two earlier, Daniel Ellsberg—perhaps the most extreme of the "repentant hawks" spawned by Vietnam —returned to the Berkeley campus, scene of so many demonstrations against the war, and told an audience of students there that submitting to registration would be an act comparable to the blind faith demanded of the Reverend Jim Jones's followers in Guyana. "Thrice-born Jimmy Carter is reborn again as Jim Jones," he said. "We all live in Guyana now." [2] And at Princeton, other students demonstrated against registration with such slogans as "Are a few barrels of oil worth the shedding of a drop of blood?" "We won't fight for Exxon," and "There is nothing worth dying for" [3] (an attitude they might well have learned from Joseph Heller and that Nietzsche once identified as the mark of a slave).

11 · Anti-Americanism Today

FOREMOST among the things not worth dying for from this point of view is the United States of America. Obviously the explicit anti-Americanism which surfaced on the radical Left in the late sixties and spilled over into the seventies has receded. No longer do we see the name of the country spelled as *Amerika* to suggest an association with Nazi Germany. Nor do vilifications of American society fill the papers and the airwaves as they did only a few years ago. Most of the radicals are either gone or transformed. Eldridge Cleaver has become a born-again Christian and a patriot. Rennie Davis has become an insurance salesman. Tom Hayden has joined the Democratic party. Jerry Rubin is off the streets and "into" the pursuit of maturity. Abbie Hoffman has disappeared. But this does not mean that the anti-American attitudes they and others like them did so much to propagate have also disappeared. These attitudes are still here and, in the subtler shapes they now assume, are perhaps even more widespread, and certainly more respectable, than they ever were before.

They are present, for example, in the still current idea that the main obstacle to nuclear disarmament is the American military establishment and that unilateral reductions by the United States are all that is needed to make the Soviets follow suit. They are present in the idea that Americans consume more than their "fair share" of resources and that a voluntary reduction in the American standard of living (a kind of unilateral economic disarmament) is all that is needed to facilitate a more equitable distribution of wealth around the world. And they are present in the notion that the United States is the guilty party in every situation that arises. It is our fault that the Khmer Rouge murdered nearly half the population of Cambodia (because we drove them to desperate measures); it is our fault that the hostages were taken in Iran (because we supported the Shah for so many years); it is even our fault that the Soviets invaded Afghanistan (because by questioning the SALT treaty and taking steps to strengthen our defenses, we simultaneously frightened them and removed their incentive to restraint).

In this fashion—to cite the words of the great Yugoslav dissident Milovan Djilas—has the United States "added moral disarmament to its puzzling eagerness to throw away its arms at the first sound of a softly spoken Soviet word." [1]

12 · The New Isolationism

THIS SPECIES of anti-American feeling, as Robert W. Tucker has pointed out,[1] stands in the sharpest possible contrast to isolationism in its traditional form, which took the view that the United States, the New Jerusalem, would be corrupted by the "entangling alliances" George Washington had warned against. But if this older variant of isolationism believed that the United States was too good to play a role in international affairs, the new isolationism of the post-Vietnam period believes that we are not good enough—that, indeed, we are a force for evil, a menace, a terror. It is thus hard to distinguish from simple anti-Americanism.

There is, however, another strain of the new isolationism which is given neither to the moral chauvinism of the past nor to the self-hatred of the present. This particular strain also grew out of Vietnam in the form of a revulsion against the entire policy of containment of which Vietnam itself had been the culmination. As such, it brought liberals and conservatives together into an alliance that scarcely dared speak its name—so dirty a word had "isolationism" become in the American political vocabulary through its association in the 1930's with the forces that were unwilling to join in the struggle against Hitler.

In the case of many conservatives—particularly in the business community—the idea began to take hold that the foreign policy we had been pursuing since 1947 was now hurting the dollar, weakening our competitive position in international trade, and in general damaging the economy. Might the answer not lie in getting out of the business of trying to hold the Communists back and getting into the business of trying to sell them goods? In the case of the liberals, the same idea was given a different twist in the demand for a "reordering of priorities" from an emphasis on foreign affairs to a new concentration on our social problems at home.

For the conservatives, the new attitudes came to a head in a degree of support for "détente" with the Soviet Union and the opening to Communist China that would once have been considered astonishing in such traditionally anti-Communist political quarters. But of course there was also a long tradition in the American business community of servicing or trying to service the Soviet market (an effort Lenin once described as selling the Soviets the rope with which they would hang the sellers). The economic "linkages" built into this new relation to the Communist world were thus as much an incentive to the American business community as to the Russians and the Chinese.

As for the liberals, their new isolationism came to an even more dramatic head shortly after the 1972 election in an attack on the powers of the presidency; and subsequent to that, in a campaign against the CIA— that is, against, respectively, the main instrument for conducting an overt policy of containment and the main instrument for conducting a covert policy of containment.

To be sure, containment was not the issue explicitly or perhaps even consciously raised by the Watergate and CIA investigations. Yet it is hard to believe that liberals would have mounted an offensive against "the imperial presidency" or the CIA at a time when they were still enthusiastic about countering—to quote John F. Kennedy's words again—"indirect non-overt aggression, intimidation and subversion, internal revolution." Indeed, the presidency would never have grown to "imperial" proportions without the encouragement and support of liberals, who encouraged and supported it precisely (though not exclusively—there were also domestic considerations) because such a presidency was necessary to the carrying out of a strategy of containment. So, too, with the CIA, which was as much a liberal creation as "the imperial presidency" and whose political tone a large number of liberals—including scholars, writers, and trade unionists—had found sufficiently congenial as recently as the mid-sixties.

Would the liberals have mounted an offensive against the powers of the presidency if one of their own had been sitting in the White House in 1972? Perhaps; the isolationist current had grown very strong by then among liberals, it was pressing hard for institutional change, and the obvious first target was the presidency. Fortunately for the liberals, however, the office was now occupied not by a Kennedy or even by a Johnson, but by their ancient enemy, Richard Nixon, a man they detested with a passion matched in living memory only by the hatred of Wall Street for Franklin Delano Roosevelt. Like Roosevelt, Nixon was forging a new coalition which, there was good reason to fear after the 1972 landslide, might freeze the liberals out of the White House for as long as the New Deal coalition had frozen the conservatives out in an earlier day. The liberals would therefore have had every incentive to go after Nixon even if an attack on the powers of the presidency had not been demanded by their deepening isolationist mood. As it was, they were presented with an opportunity to wreak vengeance on the person of Richard Nixon, to improve their future political prospects, and at the same time to dissociate themselves entirely from the very presidential prerogatives that they had formerly helped to establish and justify but that now no longer suited either their political interests or their new political beliefs.

It is no wonder that the liberals should have seized on such an opportunity. But it will always be a great and impenetrable wonder that Nixon cooperated—by acquiescing in the pointless break-in of the Democratic offices in the Watergate, by participating in the cover-up, by first taping his own incriminating conversations and then failing to destroy the tapes while he still had time to do so. Nevertheless, cooperate Nixon did, and he, who had originally risen to national prominence through the exploitation of a congressional investigating committee, was now destroyed by exactly the same instrument, but to exactly the opposite effect. In exposing Alger Hiss as a Soviet agent, Congressman Richard Nixon had made a major contribution to the bringing home of the Soviet threat and therefore to the mobilization of popular support for a foreign policy designed to counter it. In being exposed as an abuser of the public trust, President Richard Nixon made a major contribution to the weakening of the single most important institutional instrument for the execution of just such a policy and therefore to the entrenchment of the new isolationism.

The campaign against the CIA was an equally vivid case of dramatic reversal. In fact, the entire episode was like a replay of the days when committees in both the House and the Senate were investigating the activities of the Communist party—especially its underground activities—and when anti-Communist staff members and other bureaucrats leaked a daily diet of sensational revelations to an entirely complaisant and uncritical press. Now the same thing was happening, but this time it was an agency of our own government that was in the dock, investigated by both houses of Congress, exposed and held up to public scorn by the media, harassed by private vigilante groups, and portrayed as virtually unlimited in its power to harm. The Communist once supposed to be under every American bed was now replaced by a CIA agent, and the very people who had once ridiculed this exaggerated idea of Communist infiltration into American life saw nothing paranoid in analogous fantasies about the CIA.

Abuses were another matter, for the CIA had undoubtedly been guilty of abuses. But then so had there undoubtedly been Communists working in the State Department in the days of McCarthyism—and no more than merely purging the Department of its few Communist employees had seemed the true purpose of McCarthyism did cleaning up these abuses seem to be the animating passion of the liberal attack on the CIA. While there was much pious talk both in Congress and in the press about reforming the CIA, there was also much—unmistakably more sincere—talk among liberals about restricting it to the gathering of information and destroying its ability (through statute or strict congressional oversight) to conduct covert operations of any kind against the spread of Communism. For if what McCarthyism did was mobilize support for an anti-Communist foreign policy by making the danger of Communism seem domestic and immediate, the attack on the CIA was conversely bound to help demobilize support for an anti-Communist foreign policy by representing such a policy not only as a threat to the freedom and independence of other countries, but also as a sinister danger to American liberties here at home.

The new liberal isolationists, then, in their campaign against "the imperial presidency," first damaged the main institutional capability the United States possesses for conducting an overt policy of containment; and then, in their campaign against the CIA, they helped reduce the main American institutional capability for conducting a covert policy of containment.

In the wake of Iran and Afghanistan, the new isolationism has receded but it has by no means disappeared. Its institutional heritage of a weakened presidency and a crippled CIA remains, and the influence of its accompanying attitudes can still be felt among conservatives and liberals alike.

Among conservatives it surfaced, for example, in what to anyone unaware of its hold on the business community would have seemed the altogether paradoxical refusal of every Republican candidate for the presidency —even those, like John Connally, whose rhetoric was belligerently anti-Soviet and anti-Communist—to support the grain and technology embargoes announced by the President after the invasion of Afghanistan. And the liberal variety was much in evidence in expressions of alarm over the introduction of a bill to free the CIA from some of the restrictions that had been hampering its operations, and in laments over the starving of domestic needs by a voracious military establishment.

There is no necessary logical connection among anti-Americanism, isolationism, and the tendency to explain away or even apologize for anything the Soviet Union does, no matter how menacing, as nonthreatening to us. But certainly there is a psychological connection. After all, if renouncing our responsibility to hold the line against Soviet power means that we ourselves (not to mention others to whom we have made commitments) are placed in jeopardy, the case for isolationism becomes very much less appealing. Accordingly, in answer to the question "Does Afghanistan Matter?" Ronald Steel (the biographer of Walter Lippmann) declares: "Obviously not. Not in terms of any vital American interest,. that is." [2] While piously deploring the Soviet invasion, Dave Dellinger, who became well known as a leader of the antiwar movement in the sixties, tells a rally at Yale that "the greater threat to world peace" comes from "the reaction of President Carter, the press, and the Presidential candidates" to it.[3] And George Kennan, in a widely echoed sentiment, asserts that the real danger to our security arises not from a "Soviet military threat that remains to be proved" but from ourselves: "If the Persian Gulf is really vital to our security, it is surely we who, by our unrestrained greed for oil, have made it so." [4]

Even some influential commentators who are not isolationists or "semi-isolationists" and who do not reflexively blame the United States for everything evil that happens in the world often interpret Soviet behavior in ways calculated to minimize American alarm. The Soviets, they tell us, are not really expansionist and certainly not out to dominate the world; all they want is to protect their own borders and their own security. Even the invasion of Afghanistan itself has been interpreted by several such commentators not as a sign of Soviet aggressiveness but as a symptom of Soviet weakness (in contrast, presumably, to the strength the United States showed in begging the UN and the World Court to do something about Iran).

A striking instance is Arthur Schlesinger, Jr. In the forties and fifties, when the Soviet Union was very much weaker than the United States, Schlesinger expressed great anxiety over the Soviet threat; yet now, when the Soviet Union is at least as powerful as we are and by any objective standard constitutes a greater threat, he tells us how beleaguered and toothless the Russians have become:

Our hard-liners like to think that the Soviet Union is a dynamic and purposeful state following a policy laid down with consistency, foresight and coherence. But it may as well be that the Soviet Union is a weary, drab country, led by sick old men, beset by insuperable problems at home and abroad and living from crisis to crisis. It may well have invaded Afghanistan out of weakness, not out of strength, for reasons that are essentially defensive rather than aggressive, local rather than global, despairing rather than joyously premeditated.[5]

13 · Thinking About the Unthinkable Again

THIS malevolent legacy of the war in Vietnam, this combination of pacifism, anti-Americanism, and isolationism, is the most potent of all the forces working against the reawakening of an American resolve to resist the forward surge of Soviet imperialism. Beyond and apart from the particular legacy of Vietnam, moreover, is yet another factor—the fear of a nuclear holocaust.

Even before Afghanistan, the debate over SALT II had generated a whole new wave of articulated horror over the prospect of nuclear war; after Afghanistan, the wave began to swell. Citing the need to counter what Anthony Lewis in *The New York Times* characterized as "a general surge of hawkishness, of strident talk about war, . . . a new tendency to talk in a matter-of-fact way about the use of nuclear weapons," an organization called Physicians for Social Responsibility held a two-day symposium in Cambridge, Massachusetts, on the medical consequences of nuclear weapons. "The audience listened in dead silence" as Dr. Howard H. Hiatt,

the dean of the Harvard School of Public Health, described the hideous effects of a single nuclear weapon on the
Boston area. ("Of the 3 million people living in the
Boston metropolitan area, 2.2 million would be killed
at once by the blast or fire storm. Of the survivors, Dr.
Hiatt said, many 'are badly burned, blinded and otherwise seriously wounded. Many are disoriented. These
are the short-term effects; the problem of radiation sick-
ness will grow.' " Etc.) [1]

Around the same time, *The New Yorker* magazine
ran two morbidly eloquent editorials in two successive
issues on the consequences of nuclear war, which, it
asserted, would be the inevitable outcome of "the first
shot . . . fired between American and Soviet troops." [2]

That nuclear war would be a calamity beyond measure hardly needs to be stressed. But something does
need to be said about the political meaning of this kind
of talk—and Djilas said it even before the invasion of
Afghanistan:

. . . the West has inflicted certain psychological wounds on
itself which have no parallel in the Soviet Union. I have
especially in mind the anti-nuclear propaganda of the Western Left. Their constant harping on mega-deaths and the
prospect of doom descending on us unless SALT is signed,
sealed and ratified has a debilitating impact on the NATO
countries and especially on the United States. A few weeks
before SALT 2 was signed, the US Congressional Office of
Technology Assessment (of all places) saw fit to publish a
blood-curdling scenario of what America would be like after
a few atomic blasts: "Areas of the country such as the North-
east corridor were reduced to a swath of burning rubble from
north of Boston to the south of Norfolk," and so on.
Cui bono? The answer is obvious. No such accounts of the

horrors of nuclear war ever reach the Soviet public, because the whole area of military planning is banned from discussion. This means that in the vital field of psychological confrontation the balance is strongly tilted in favor of Soviet interests. Some of the sentiments one hears expressed in the White House on this and similar topics would make fine Sunday-morning sermons in a little village community—but can they seriously be meant as America's response to Soviet policies? [3]

14 · The Culture of Appeasement

In thinking about all this, I have been struck very forcibly, as many others have been too, by certain resemblances between the United States in the post-Vietnam period and Great Britain in the years after the First World War. The British, of course, were on the winning side in that war, whereas we were the losers in Vietnam. But World War I took so great a toll of lives and ideals that for all practical purposes it was experienced by the British as a defeat. Especially among the upper-class young—as Martin Green shows in his brilliant "Narrative of 'Decadence' in England After 1918," *Children of the Sun*[1]—there developed many of the same tendencies we see all around us in America today. Thus, for example, words such as "soldier" and "fighting," which had previously carried a positive charge, now became so distasteful that the *Iliad*, with its celebration of the martial virtues, could no longer be comfortably read. Nothing good could be said about war: it was wanton carnage pure and simple. Nor was it ever justified; the things that matter, Aldous Huxley declared, can be neither defended nor imposed by force of arms. When war comes, wrote Brian Howard in verse more typical in its sentiments than gifted in its language, it is "because a parcel of damned old men/Want some fun or some power or something." It was in an atmosphere suffused with such ideas and attitudes that the Oxford Pledge never to fight "for King and country" was taken by so many thousands of British undergraduates in the early 1930's.

For England itself had been discredited by the First World War in the eyes of an entire generation of the privileged young. It was a wicked country because it had senselessly sent the flower of its youth to the slaughter, and it was doomed because it rested on obsolescent social and political foundations (by which some meant that there was too much inequality and others meant there was not enough). Worst of all from the point of view of not a few of these "bright young things" of the postwar period, England was dull and philistine. The arts were more exciting in France and life was more interesting in Germany. England was in fact so stodgy in its tastes, so puritanical in its morals, and so drearily middle class in its culture that almost any alternative society was to be preferred.

Politically this hostility to England could find expression equally well on the Left and the Right. Perhaps the most striking example was the Mitford sisters, daughters of the country's highest aristocracy, one of whom, Unity, became a Nazi and another, Jessica, became a Communist. The story is told of a British diplomat who was set upon by the two sisters during a visit to their country estate in the early thirties. Are you, they demanded of him, " 'a Fascist or a Communist?' and I said, 'Neither, I'm a democrat.' Whereupon they answered, 'How wet.' " [2]

There were a good many others in the upper reaches of British society who also thought that being a democrat was "wet" (or as I suppose we would say today, square). Some, like Sir Oswald Mosley and his followers in the British Union of Fascists, as well as prominent writers like D. H. Lawrence and Wyndham Lewis, sympathized with or actually supported Hitler and Mussolini (Osbert Sitwell, anticipating a similar fantasy of today about Italian Communism as a "third force," once argued that Italian fascism offered an escape from the equally horrible alternatives of Russian Bolshevism and American capitalism); others, like W. H. Auden, Stephen Spender, John Strachey, and Philip Toynbee, were attracted to Stalin and to Communism. And there were even some for whom being a democrat was so wet that they were willing to commit treason against the democratic country in which they lived. About treason, at least, there was nothing wet. Whereas "to many English people," Rebecca West later wrote, patriotism had "something dowdy about it," treason had "a certain style, a sort of elegance." [3] Moreover, it was understandable that treason should be committed against England. Thus when Guy Burgess, who had been a Soviet agent while pretending to work for British Intelligence, fled to Moscow in the fifties just as he was about to be caught, Auden said that his old friend had become a Russian citizen for the same reason that he himself had become an American citizen—"it was the only way completely and finally to rebel against England." [4]

One wonders: to what extent did the policy of appeasing Hitler which the British government followed in the thirties derive from the fear that a generation raised on pacifism and contempt for the life of its own society would refuse or be unable to resist so powerful and self-confident an enemy as Nazi Germany? It would be very hard to say, although we know that at least one prominent Englishman of the day, the press magnate Lord Rothermere, believed that "a moribund people such as ours is not equipped to deal with a totalitarian state." [5] We know, too, that Hitler himself thought the British would never fight. As he went from strength to strength, they seemed to grow more and more fearful. Except for a few lonely figures like Winston Churchill, who were generally dismissed by their own countrymen as hysterical warmongers, they blinded themselves to his intentions, rationalizing away his every aggressive move and proclaiming that every advance he made was bringing the world closer and closer to peace. What else could this mean but that they had already given up?

It is of the greatest interest to note that Brezhnev has expressed similar sentiments about the United States. A few years ago, in a speech to Communist party leaders in Prague—to which as little attention has been paid in this country as was paid in England to equally revealing speeches by Hitler in the 1930's—Brezhnev bragged of the advances the Soviet Union had been making under cover of détente and predicted that they would lead to an irreversible shift in the balance of power by the 1980's. One imagines that he was led to this conclusion by the response of the United States to the Soviet military build-up, a response which has uncannily followed the pattern of British response to the German build-up of the thirties.

Walter Laqueur [6] divides the British response into four distinct stages. In stage one, it was claimed that the reports of German rearmament were grossly exaggerated; in stage two, the reports were acknowledged as true, but it was alleged that Germany was so far behind that it would never catch up; in stage three, it was admitted that Germany had achieved parity with or even surpassed Britain, but it was also said that this did not constitute a military threat since the Germans had to defend themselves against potential enemies in the East as well as in the West; and in stage four, when the full extent of German superiority was finally faced, it was said that survival now had to be the overriding consideration, and the counsels of appeasement prevailed.

Compare this to the description by Harvard's Richard Pipes (who also headed a team of nongovernmental experts appointed during the Ford administration to review the CIA's estimate of Soviet military capability) of the American response to the Soviet military build-up of the past few years: "The frenetic pace of the Soviet nuclear build-up was explained first on the ground that the Russians had a lot of catching up to do, then that they had to consider the Chinese threat, and finally on the grounds that they are inherently a very insecure people and should be allowed an edge in deterrent capability." [7]

Churchill, thinking of the ancient adage *si vis pacem*

para bellum ("If you want peace, prepare for war"), later called World War II "the unnecessary war." It could, he thought, have been prevented if the democracies had rearmed earlier instead of allowing the military balance to tip in Hitler's favor. But the culture of appeasement created a situation in which rearmament became impossible. At the time it seemed that the German incorporation of Austria in 1938 might finally turn the tide of British opinion, but Churchill correctly foresaw that not even so vivid a demonstration of Hitler's expansionist purposes would disturb the complacency of the appeasers:

Very likely this immediate crisis will pass, will dissipate itself and calm down. After a boa constrictor has devoured its prey, it often has a considerable digestive spell. . . . If there is a pause then people will be saying, "See how the alarmists have been confronted, Europe has calmed down, it has all but blown over, the tension is greatly relaxed." . . . The *Times* will write a leading article to say how silly those people look who raised a clamor for exceptional action in foreign policy and defense, and how wise it was not to be carried away by this passing incident. . . .[8]

Thus, by inexorable consequence, did war become the only alternative to surrender.

Is the same thing happening to us today? There is abundant reason to think that it is. Secretary of State Cyrus Vance assures the world, weeks after the invasion of Afghanistan, that "we seek no return of the cold war" and then goes on to denigrate the containment policy of the past as "the indiscriminate confrontation of earlier times." [9] A major American political leader like Senator Edward Kennedy declares, in an eerie echo of the poem by Brian Howard I quoted above, that "We should not be moving toward the brink of sending another generation of the young to die for the failures of the old." [10] Other echoes of the thirties in England are sounded in important periodicals like *The New York Times* ("Once the dust settles, America should initiate specific actions to reduce tensions and in the meantime do nothing to make that more difficult when the time comes" [11]) and *The New Yorker* ("Since avoidance of nuclear destruction is the greatest interest that any nation could have, why is it that when we are brought face to face with it we grow silent instead of seeking some diplomatic way out of the impasse?" [12]). Placards inscribed with slogans like "There is nothing worth dying for" are carried by sociological and spiritual descendants of those aristocratic British students of the thirties who vowed never to fight for king and country (for example, Mark Waren, graduate of "an exclusive academy on New York's Upper East Side," son of two college professors, and now studying at Princeton [13]).

Hearing and reading and seeing all this, one finds it easy to think that we are moving beyond stage three in the culture of appeasement and into stage four where surrender or war are the only remaining choices. One finds it easy to think this, and one finds it easy to despair.

15 · The New Nationalism

ᴀɴᴅ ʏᴇᴛ, and yet. If on the one hand the soporific forces among us remain powerful, there is on the other hand a contrary tendency, and a very strong one, which has also been developing in the United States alongside the culture of appeasement. It is a tendency toward what might be called a new nationalism, and it carries with it the main hope we now have for saving ourselves from the alternatives of war or Finlandization that an unimpeded culture of appeasement is certain in the end to yield.

The new nationalism made its first significant appearance in 1972, when widespread disgust with the negative attitudes toward American power in the world, expressed by the "new politics" movement behind George McGovern's candidacy and by McGovern himself ("Come Home, America"), enabled even so unpopular a politician as Richard Nixon to win reelection by the second-largest margin in American history. A few years later it surfaced once more in the overwhelming public approval of then UN ambassador Daniel P. Moynihan's declarations of the moral superiority of the United States and its political culture to its critics and enemies both in the Communist bloc and in the Third World. It burst out again during the bicentennial celebrations in 1976. And of course it reached the dimensions of a tidal wave in response to the taking of the hostages in Iran. Of its many expressions, my own favorite was the comment of an administrator at San Diego State University, a survivor of the campus rallies of the sixties, as he watched a self-described "pro-American rally" that drew eight hundred students at SDSU: "I never thought," he said happily, "I would live to see this day." [1]

The San Diego administrator would have been less surprised if he had been paying closer attention to what was happening in the United States. For just as the new mood had been building before the taking of the hostages, it had also been assuming more tangible forms than the waving of flags or the shouting of slogans. For example, support for increased spending on defense had been rising steadily since 1971 and had already reached a record high of 60 percent before the Iranian crisis erupted.[2] A parallel increase of support for the use of force in defense of American interests had also been showing up in the survey data during the same period.[3] And long before Iran, the debate over SALT II was revealing a degree of anxiety over the slippage of American power in relation to the Soviet Union that amazed even some critics of the treaty who had been denounced as cold warriors and Pentagon apologists for pointing to the facts of the case only a few years ago.

To some extent, the new nationalism represented a

normal swing of the pendulum—in this instance away from the hostility toward America that became so prevalent during the late sixties and early seventies. The ideas associated with this anti-American upsurge—that the United States was a sick society and a force for evil in international affairs—had for some years been coming under very effective fire from a group of intellectuals often labeled "neoconservative" but who might more accurately have been described as "neonationalists" in line with their highly positive view of the values implicit in the constitutional and institutional structure of American civilization and their belief that the survival of liberty and democracy requires a forceful American presence in the world.

In part, the "neoconservatives" became influential simply because they were able to best their opponents in argument. But they were certainly helped along by a series of events that eroded the foundations of the anti-American case. Thus the idea that the American role in Vietnam had been immoral or criminal became harder and harder to maintain in the face of the horrors the Communists began visiting upon the peoples of Indochina following the defeat of the American effort to prevent Communist domination of that region. Similarly, the idea that the United States was the cause of the nuclear arms race—that the Soviet Union was only strengthening its nuclear arsenal in response to us —became harder and harder to argue as the Soviet Union was permitted by the United States to achieve parity and then began pushing forward toward superiority.

In the end, the new nationalism may or may not prevail against the culture of appeasement. But whatever

the eventual outcome of the literally fateful struggle between these two forces, the new nationalism is clearly
neither insubstantial nor evanescent. It will not easily
be dissipated and politicians will ignore it, if they do,
only at extreme peril to their chances at the polls.

Therefore, at the very least, before it runs its course,
a variety of steps will be taken to strengthen our military capabilities. As "No More Vietnams" meant retrenchment and accommodation, "No More Irans" will
mean making sure that we never again have to submit
helplessly to being "pushed around"; and as the main
"Lesson of Vietnam" was taken to be that we must
never again intervene into the Third World, the great
"Lesson of Afghanistan" is likely to be that unless we
intervene under certain circumstances, we will find ourselves at the mercy of our enemies.

16 · The Missing Term

In MY JUDGMENT, even if the new lessons were to go no further than they have already gone, they would constitute progress toward a healthier and a safer America. Healthier because self-respect is spiritually superior to self-flagellation, in nations no less than in individuals; safer because the determination to defend our own interests will make us more secure than the inclination to appease.

Nevertheless, something is still missing from the new nationalism. In the immediate aftermath of Iran, there was a good deal of talk about defending American honor. Since Afghanistan, most of the talk, in the streets, in the speeches, and in the official statements alike, has focused on defending our economic interests. That there is a political dimension to this crisis, that something more is at stake than injured pride or access to oil, no one seems to recognize, or at any rate to emphasize. What this suggests is that the general American response to Iran and Afghanistan, while marking an end to the period of American retreat, has not yet carried us fully forward into a new period of containment.

The problem is that a key term has quietly disappeared from the discussion of the Soviet-American conflict. It is the term "Communism." One would think from most of what has been said in recent months that the Soviet Union is a nation like any other, with which we are in competition. Not once in President Carter's State of the Union address of 1980—the very speech announcing the Carter Doctrine—does the word "Communism" even appear; and in two lengthy analyses of the speech, one by Stanley Hoffmann[1] and the other by Leslie H. Gelb,[2] the word is used a total of three times, but only to be dismissed as insignificant. Yet if the Soviet Union really were a nation like any other—if it were, for example, still being ruled by the czars—would we object to the extension of its power over the Persian Gulf? What difference would it make to us? Would we be worse off buying oil from the czars than buying it from the sheiks? Might we not even prefer such an arrangement (as indeed the letter in the *Times* from which I quoted earlier does even now)?

We might, though even under those circumstances we would have cause for serious concern. But as it is, and to give us cause for infinitely more serious concern, the Soviet Union is not a nation like any other. It is a revolutionary state, exactly as Hitler's Germany was, in the sense that it wishes to create a new international order in which it would be the dominant power and whose character would be determined by its national wishes and its ideological dictates. In such an order there would be no more room for any of the freedoms or the prosperity we now enjoy than there is at this moment within the Soviet Union, or any of the other Communist countries.

For Communism, whether dominated by Moscow or not, has been a curse. To this day there is not a single Communist country in the world in which even the mildest criticism of the government, not verbal and most certainly not organizational, is permitted. Nor can novelists and poets write or composers compose or painters paint as they wish and what they wish. To be sure, people are no longer shot or imprisoned with such orgiastic promiscuity in the Soviet Union as they were during the forty years when (according to Solzhenitsyn's estimate) some *sixty million* persons were "secretly done to death by exhaustion, . . . frozen to death in uninhabited wastes, [and] decimated by famine," [3] untold millions of them *political* prisoners in the system of camps he calls the Gulag Archipelago—people whose only crime, that is, was opposition or even suspected opposition to the regime. Yet neither can Soviet citizens today speak their minds in public, let alone organize politically, without being exiled or thrown into jails or insane asylums where they are "cured" of their irrational ideas and then released or deported.

These conditions are not confined to the Soviet Union; they obtain in every country that has had the misfortune to be forced to live under Communism—and there is still not a single case of any people freely choosing to live under it. "When," Senator Moynihan has asked, "was the last time anyone can remember a refugee swimming through shark-infested waters, or a boatload braving the high seas, in order to reach the secure shores of East Germany or Cuba?"[4] The one Communist government that has ever come to power through the polls did so in Chile, where the "Marxists" under Allende received about 35 percent of the vote and then proceeded to alienate the population by wrecking the economy—which was then of course blamed on the machinations of the CIA.

This record is consistent with the abysmal economic performance of Communist governments everywhere, emphatically including the Soviet Union. After more than sixty years of Communist rule, the only thing the Soviets seem to be good at is producing nuclear bombs and missiles. The Soviet Union is still unable to feed itself despite vast expanses of fertile land, and it still has to apply to the United States for technological help in developing other industries. Not only, then, do they destroy liberty and humane culture wherever their writ extends ("A curse on all Bolsheviks," said the great Bolshevik Leon Trotsky himself, "they bring a dryness and a hardness into life"), the Communists do not even make good on their promise to improve the material lot of the people. No wonder it is mordantly said in East Europe that under Soviet domination, the Sahara would experience a shortage of sand.

Nor do the Communists make good on their claim to serve the value of equality—the prime value of their political culture. Everywhere they begin by dispossessing and murdering the older ruling classes (in Cambodia, they ordered the evacuation of all the cities within twenty-four hours, driving some four-and-a-half million people, including infants, graybeards, and invalids, into the countryside at gunpoint to die of starvation and

93

disease or scratch out a dubious living from the earth;
and special care was taken to kill everyone who was
literate or suspected of being so on the basis of such
telltale evidence as the mere possession of a pair of eye-
glasses). But as Djilas and others have shown, everywhere the old inequalities of class and rank and status
are gradually reintroduced. Djilas:

> ... the vast majority in the Soviet Union are poor or very
> poor, while a small minority lord it over the majority in vary-
> ing states of relative or even absolute affluence.
>
> And why has all this arisen? Because Soviet society is
> egalitarian *in theory*, but no one has the freedom to raise his
> voice in protest when vague egalitarianism is reversed into
> crude exploitation.
>
> Western society does not claim to be egalitarian, and isn't;
> but it is intellectually and socially free. This means that the
> grosser forms of inequality and abuse in earning power, social
> benefits, and the like are kept under public scrutiny so that
> injustices are identified and kept within limits. The end re-
> sult is that Western "capitalist" society is now socially more
> just than Soviet society; and income in Western society is in-
> comparably more fairly distributed than under the Soviet
> system. Literally as well as symbolically, it *pays* to be free.[5]

In short, the reason Soviet imperialism is a threat to
us is not merely that the Soviet Union is a superpower
bent on aggrandizing itself, but that it is a Communist state armed, as Sakharov says, to the teeth, and
dedicated to the destruction of the free institutions
which are our heritage and the political culture which
is our glory. For Communism, Solzhenitsyn writes, "can
implement its 'ideals' only by destroying the core and
foundations of a nation's life." And yet: "All warnings

to the West about the pitiless and insatiable nature of Communist regimes have proved to be in vain because the acceptance of such a view would be too terrifying. . . . Most amazing is that the Communists themselves have for decades loudly proclaimed their goal of destroying the bourgeois world (they have become more circumspect lately), while the West merely smiled at what seemed to be an extravagant joke." [6]

To the majestic moral witness of Solzhenitsyn on the subject of how the West has responded to Communism in general, Djilas adds his special intellectual authority on the subject of how it has responded to the Soviet Union in particular:

What our five senses tell us is that, whether with brute force or without—with military occupation or without—Soviet hegemony has been gradually expanding in all parts of the world. . . . What our five senses also tell us is that the Western nations appear to be totally unprepared and even . . . unwilling to say to the Russians: This is where you are going to stop! [7]

17 · "This Implacable Challenge"

In 1947, George F. Kennan called Soviet expansionism an "implacable challenge" to the United States and to "the free institutions of the Western world." Today, when the United States has lost the preponderance of power it enjoyed then and the balance is shifting in favor of the Soviet Union, the danger is far greater and the challenge even more implacable. Do we have the will to reverse the decline of American power and to resist the forward surge of Soviet imperialism today as we did in 1947? To resist, if we are to resist, will demand today, as it did in 1947, that we recognize Soviet purposes for what they are. It is tragic that Kennan himself, in 1980, should be among those working to prevent such a recognition. Writing of the invasion of Afghanistan,[1] he condemns the "extravagant view of Soviet motivation" according to which this "ill-considered" Soviet action was "a prelude to aggressive military moves against various countries and regions further afield." The American response he dismisses as "strident"—a case of "warning people publicly not to do things they have never evinced any intention of doing." Most astonishing of all, Kennan tells us that he is "not aware of any substantiation" of the extravagant American view "in anything the Soviet leaders themselves had said or done."

If he is really looking for substantiation, I would advise him to begin by reading his own essay on "The Sources of Soviet Conduct," which, though written over thirty years ago, tells us more about the invasion of Afghanistan than the sorry article Kennan produced a few weeks after the invasion actually took place. The Kennan of 1980 sees the invasion as merely defensive: has not Brezhnev himself characterized it thus? The Kennan of 1947 would have understood that the invasion represents a new stage in what he described then as the unremitting "Soviet pressure against the free institutions of the Western world."

Of course, in defining our conflict with the Soviet Union as a struggle for freedom and against Communism, we run into two great questions. The first concerns China. If Communism is the enemy, why should we be aligning ourselves with China, the other great Communist power? The answer given by supporters of the "China card" is the same justification that was used for the free world's alliance with one totalitarian ruler, Stalin, against another, Hitler, who was at that moment more dangerous. It is a reasonable answer. The problem, however, is that whereas Stalin made a major contribution to the defeat of Hitler, Communist China is so weak that its contribution to the containment of Soviet imperialism may be negligible. In order to keep forty Soviet divisions pinned down on the Chinese border—

divisions the Soviet build-up has made it possible for them to spare—we may be helping to turn China into a terror to our children and grandchildren. And since China's only interest in us is protection from the Soviet Union, if we rely on the China card as an excuse for failing to build up our own power, we may at the same time find ourselves promoting what we tell ourselves we most fear: a Sino-Soviet rapprochement.

Another price of the China card is the loss of political clarity it inevitably entails. Playing one Communist power off against another may be sound geopolitics, but it increases the difficulty of explaining to ourselves and our friends what we are fighting for and what we are fighting against. It may therefore make it harder to mobilize the political support without which a steady and consistent strategy of containment is impossible.

This problem of mobilizing support is perhaps even more difficult in Western Europe and Japan than it is in the United States. By voting for Carter in the Democratic caucuses even after his announcement of an embargo on the export of their grain to the Soviet Union, the farmers of Iowa have already shown that they can see beyond their economic interests, but the French, the West Germans, and the Japanese seem to care only, as Jacobo Timerman (the well-known Argentine newspaper editor now living in Israel) puts it,[2] about "the orderly supply and consumption of raw materials and the inviolability of their markets." Thus trade agreements between the Soviet Union and the West, which were supposed to create incentives to Soviet moderation, have evidently worked in the opposite direction so far as Western Europe and Japan are concerned. The Soviets have not been restrained by the cut-off of wheat, but the French and the West Germans have hesitated to back even the relatively mild measures the President has taken against the Soviet Union. Many European commentators—Bernard Levin,[3] Jean-François Revel,[4] and Olivier Todd,[5] to name a few—see this as yet another sign that the process of self-Finlandization has gone much further in Europe than in the United States. But believing as most of them do that the chief cause of self-Finlandization is the fear of Soviet power and the concomitant loss of confidence in American resolve, they also think that a serious new assertion of American will and American power might lead to a reversal of the process and the beginning of a new determination in the other democracies to resist what Revel calls "the totalitarian temptation."

The other great question that inevitably arises in this connection is how we can speak of defending a "free world" that includes so many dictatorships of the Right. This is by now an old question, going back to the fifties. Listing the non-free countries with which we were allied in the fight against Communism became a drearily familiar refrain in the polemics of those days, reaching its climax in the sixties in the sustained assault on one South Vietnamese government after another for its offenses against liberty and democracy. How could we claim to be defending freedom or democracy when we were defending regimes like these? Surely in doing so we were showing that we were really up to something else—making the world safe for capitalism, or acting out paranoid fantasies of an imaginary Communist menace, or merely throwing our imperial weight around for its own sweet sake.

99

Yet the United States *was* leading a free-world alliance in the entirely meaningful sense that every free society in the world was either a member of the alliance or under its protection. It is true that out of prudential considerations, like the need for bases, certain authoritarian regimes and right-wing dictatorships were also included in the alliance. But in view of the fact that such associations were important in holding back the single greatest and most powerful threat to freedom on the face of the earth, they could be justified as an unfortunate political and military necessity. And even on the level of moral argument, the case could be made that the dictatorships of Franco and Salazar, or of the colonels in Greece, or of Park and Thieu, at least left room for a greater degree of freedom than the Communist countries did, and were also far more likely to be replaced in the future by democratic governments. Indeed, while there is still not a single instance of any Communist regime being overthrown and succeeded by a democratic government, Spain, Portugal, and Greece are all democratic countries today. As for South Vietnam, it has been swallowed by an infinitely more repressive regime than the Thieu government ever was or dreamed of being, and the same fate will overtake South Korea if Korea should ever be unified under the rule of the North.

In resisting the advance of Soviet power, then, we *are* fighting for freedom and against Communism, for democracy and against totalitarianism. Yet it is precisely this sense of things that the new nationalism thus far lacks. Nor does the Carter Doctrine express it with force and clarity. Without such clarity, the new nationalism is unlikely to do more than lead to sporadic outbursts of indignant energy. It cannot by itself supply the basis of support for what Kennan described in 1947 as "the adroit and vigilant application of counter-force at a series of constantly shifting geographical and political points, corresponding to the shifts and maneuvers of Soviet policy," with the ultimate hope of promoting "tendencies which must eventually find their outlet in either the breakup or the gradual mellowing of Soviet power."

The possibility that the new nationalism will prove to be a first step toward a rededication of the United States to such a strategy is what frightens Kennan himself and many others like him who have grown weary and fearful over the years. But today, in the face of the present danger, "the thoughtful observer of Russian-American relations" will no more find "cause for complaint in the Kremlin's challenge to American society" than Kennan did in 1947, when—to cite his magnificent words again—he experienced

a certain gratitude for a Providence which, by providing the American people with this implacable challenge, has made their entire security as a nation dependent on their pulling themselves together and accepting the responsibilities of moral and political leadership that history plainly intended them to bear.

In 1947 these words pointed the way to the containment of Soviet expansionism. Today, if we but consent, they can energize our resistance to Finlandization and our determination to marshal the power we will need "to assure the survival and the success of liberty" in the new and infinitely more dangerous age ahead.

Postscript to the New Edition

To bring the story told here up to date would require another book of at least equal length. But I can refer the interested reader to a number of articles I have written since the original edition of this book was published, tracking the Reagan administration's response to the present danger and the ways in which a resurgent culture of appeasement has affected that response. These articles include "The Future Danger" (*Commentary*, April 1981); "The Neoconservative Anguish over Reagan's Foreign Policy" (*New York Times Magazine*, May 2, 1982); "Appeasement by Any Other Name" (*Commentary*, July 1983); and "The Reagan Road to Détente" (*Foreign Affairs*, Vol. 63, No. 3, 1985).

ACKNOWLEDGMENTS

This book originated in a talk I gave to a meeting of the Council on Foreign Relations in Washington. I am grateful to the Council for having extended the invitation. As the editor of *Commentary*, I have also profited immensely from working with the many distinguished writers who have analyzed foreign policy in its pages during the past decade. Though none of them can be held responsible for anything in this book, they have all contributed immeasurably to it by giving me an opportunity to reflect upon, discuss, and debate the issues with some of the keenest minds that have been brought to bear on them in recent years.

Notes

1. *The Truman Doctrine and Containment*

1. Letter to the Editor by Howard L. Parsons, *The New York Times*, February 23, 1980.

2. Richard J. Walton: "Reeling Backward," op-ed, *The New York Times*, January 10, 1980.

3. Alan Wolfe: "Cold-War Windfall: Carter's Afghan Security Blanket," *The Nation*, February 2, 1980.

4. Robert Lasch: "Lessons of Korea and Vietnam," *Newsweek*, February 18, 1980.

5. Robert Lekachman: "Scoundrel Time," *The Nation*, February 16, 1980.

2. *Mr. X*

1. "Mr. X" [George F. Kennan]: "The Sources of Soviet Conduct," *Foreign Affairs*, July 1947; reprinted in G. F. Kennan: *American Diplomacy 1900–1950*, University of Chicago Press (1951).

2. *Memoirs by Harry S. Truman*, Vol. Two: *Years of Trial and Hope*, Doubleday (1956), p. 341.

3. *Enter Vietnam*

1. Richard M. Nixon: *RN: The Memoirs of Richard Nixon*, quoted in Henry Kissinger: *White House Years*, Little, Brown (1979), pp. 633–634.

2. Arthur Schlesinger, Jr.: A *Thousand Days*, Houghton Mifflin (1965), p. 307.

3. Ibid., pp. 310–311.

4. Hans J. Morgenthau: "Asia: The American Algeria," *Commentary*, July 1961, and "Vietnam—Another Korea?" *Commentary*, May 1962.

4. The Nixon Doctrine

1. "Defense Budget-Cutting," editorial, *The New York Times*, June 6, 1972.

2. "Arms and Security," editorial, *The New York Times*, October 13, 1972.

5. The Arms "Race"

1. "Missile Crisis Plus Ten," editorial, *The New York Times*, October 28, 1972.

2. "C.I.A. Finds Soviet's Arms Outlays Lead U.S. by 50%," news story by Drew Middleton, *The New York Times*, January 27, 1980.

6. "Mature Restraint"

1. Stanley Hoffmann: "Toward a Foreign Policy," op-ed, *The New York Times*, January 25, 1980.

2. James Chace: In conversation, *Straight Talk*, WOR-TV (New York), November 30, 1979.

8. The Carter Doctrine

1. "Transcript of Kennedy's Speech at Georgetown University on Campaign Issues," *The New York Times*, January 29, 1980.

2. Detailed proposals for a defense program that might be adequate to the crisis can be found in a statement by the Committee on the Present Danger (Washington) entitled "The 1980 Crisis and What We Should Do About It." Similar proposals, set forth in even greater detail, can be found in a volume edited by W. Scott Thompson under the title *From Weakness to Strength: National Security in the 1980's*, which is scheduled for publication in the spring of 1980 by the Institute for Contemporary Studies (San Francisco).

3. Op. cit., *The New York Times*, January 29, 1980.

9. *Finlandization*

1. "Russia in OPEC's Place," letter to the editor by Arthur
C. Merrill, *The New York Times*, January 27, 1980.

10. *Pacifism After Vietnam*

1. "Carter-Kennedy Clash and Unity of the Democratic
Party," news story by Steven R. Weisman, *The New York Times*,
February 15, 1980.
2. "Campus Rallies Across U.S. Protest Registration Plan,"
news story by Robert Blair Kaiser, *The New York Times*, February 13, 1980.
3. Ibid.

11. *Anti-Americanism Today*

1. George Urban: "A Conversation with Milovan Djilas,"
Encounter, December 1979, p. 37.

12. *The New Isolationism*

1. Robert W. Tucker: *A New Isolationism: Threat or Promise?*, Potomac Associates (1972), pp. 33–34.
2. Ronald Steel: "Afghanistan Doesn't Matter," *The New Republic*, February 16, 1980.
3. Kaiser, op. cit.
4. George F. Kennan: "Was This Really Mature Statesmanship?" op-ed, *The New York Times*, February 1, 1980.
5. Arthur Schlesinger, Jr.: "Is This Journey Necessary?" op-ed,
The Wall Street Journal, January 18, 1980.

13. *Thinking About the Unthinkable Again*

1. Anthony Lewis: "Thinking About the Unthinkable," op-ed, *The New York Times*, February 14, 1980.
2. "The Talk of the Town," *The New Yorker*, February 4, 1980, and February 11, 1980.
3. Urban, op. cit., p. 37.

14. *The Culture of Appeasement*

1. Martin Green: *Children of the Sun*, Basic Books (1976).
2. David Pryce-Jones, *Unity Mitford*, Dial Press/James Wade
(1977), p. 83.

3. Rebecca West: *The New Meaning of Treason*, quoted in Green, op. cit., p. 405.

4. Green, op. cit., p. 405.

5. Quoted in Walter Laqueur: "America and the World: The Next Four Years," *Commentary*, March 1977.

6. Ibid.

7. Richard Pipes: "Why the Soviet Union Thinks It Could Fight and Win a Nuclear War," *Commentary*, July 1977.

8. Quoted in Walter Laqueur: "Taking Stock of the Soviets," *The New Republic*, March 1, 1980.

9. "Vance Urging a Balanced Response on Afghanistan," news story by Bernard Gwertzman, *The New York Times*, March 4, 1980.

10. Op. cit., *The New York Times*, January 29, 1980.

11. Walton, op. cit.

12. "The Talk of the Town," *The New Yorker*, February 11, 1980.

13. "A Sign and a Conviction," news story by Robert Blair Kaiser, *The New York Times*, February 17, 1980. Evidently stung by criticism, Mr. Waren later claimed that the sign had "appeared in the march by accident," and went on to attack President Carter as "a cynical politician playing on American patriotism for personal political ends" (Letter to the editor, *The New York Times*, February 25, 1980).

15. *The New Nationalism*

1. News story, *The San Diego Union*, November 16, 1979.

2. *Public Opinion*, December/January 1980, p. 22.

3. Ibid., February/March 1980, p. 26.

16. *The Missing Term*

1. Stanley Hoffmann: "Reflections on the Present Danger," *The New York Review of Books*, March 6, 1980.

2. Leslie H. Gelb: "Beyond the Carter Doctrine," *The New York Times Magazine*, February 10, 1980.

3. Aleksandr I. Solzhenitsyn: *The Oak and the Calf*, Harper & Row (1980), p. 553. This figure has been challenged as much too high. Robert Conquest, author of the authoritative study *The Great Terror*, estimates that "the collectivization and purge deaths under Stalin"—a period about fifteen years shorter than the one

Solzhenitsyn talks about—amounted to some twenty million, though he cautions that this figure "is based on conservative assumptions at every point" ("Dear Editor," *The New Leader,* March 10, 1980).

4. Daniel P. Moynihan: Address at the City University of New York, January 16, 1980.

5. Urban, op. cit.

6. "Solzhenitsyn on Communism," *Time,* February 18, 1980.

7. Urban, op. cit.

17. *"This Implacable Challenge"*

1. Kennan, op. cit., *The New York Times,* February 1, 1980.

2. Jacobo Timerman: "Lessons of the Invasion," op-ed, *The New York Times,* February 3, 1980.

3. Bernard Levin: "As for Europe—Oh, My . . ." op-ed, *The New York Times,* January 25, 1980.

4. Jean-François Revel: *The Totalitarian Temptation,* Doubleday (1977).

5. Olivier Todd: In conversation, "America: Where Do We Go from Here?" CBS-TV, January 31, 1980.

ABOUT THE AUTHOR

Norman Podhoretz has been the editor of *Commentary* magazine since 1960. His writings have appeared in most major publications in the United States as well as in other countries throughout the world, and he is the author of a widely syndicated weekly column. Mr. Podhoretz's other books include *The Bloody Crossroads: Where Literature and Politics Meet* (1986), *Why We Were in Vietnam* (1982), *Breaking Ranks: A Political Memoir* (1979), *Making It* (1967), and *Doings and Undoings: The Fifties and After in American Writing* (1964). He lives in Manhattan with his wife, Midge Decter.